Whiskey Prayers and Midnight Moments

A Memoir of Bipolar Disorder, Addiction, and Healing

JAI Lewis

Copyright

Whiskey Prayers and Midnight Moments

First Edition 2026

Published by JAI Lewis Writes

Atlanta, Georgia

Cover design by JAI Lewis

Interior formatting by JAI Lewis

ISBN: **979-8-9953317-0-4**

Printed in the United States of America

Dedication

For My Mother –

Whose strength still colors my world. I see your favorite shade of purple in the fabric of my life. The dream is no longer a whisper — it is becoming.

Thank you for planting a pen in my spirit and teaching me that words could carry weight when my voice felt small.

For My Father –

Your steadiness shaped me. You taught me discipline, discretion, and the quiet power of endurance.

Thank you for giving me a life strong enough to build from.

For My Son –

My reason and my reminder. You are why I keep choosing forward.

You are the why beneath my becoming. I pray the life I fight for becomes the foundation you stand on. I hope this book leaves you braver, stronger, and unafraid of your own becoming.

For My Brother –

Thank you for being a steady part of my foundation.

I hope this story builds something that honors where we started — and where we are both still going.

For My Family –

Thank you for the foundation, the history, and the name I carry forward.

Twenty-five years of midnight moments.

This is the morning I named my truth.

Preface

They tried to hand me something polished.

Clinical language. Soft disclaimers. Gentle introductions.

I pushed the door open in heels.

Glossed lips. Stiff spine. Midnight still clinging to my skin.

Because this story doesn't knock politely. It enters.

With residue. With rhythm. With receipts.

There were nights I held a whiskey glass like it held answers.

Midnight pours. Whiskey-stained tears. Mascara running like truth I could no longer revise.

And there were mornings —

when that same mascara wand did more than curl lashes.

It rebuilt a woman.

Stroke by stroke.

Coating over the evidence of last night's collapse.

Turning whiskey-stained tears into something presentable.

Something employable.

Something that could walk into daylight and name itself resilience.

I mastered reconstruction.

Not the delicate kind.

The emergency kind.

This isn't a memoir about collapse.

It's about combustion.

It's about what happens when a diagnosis meets ambition.

When bipolar meets brilliance.

When anxiety shares space with intellect.

When addiction slips into the cracks and calls itself comfort.

Mental illness doesn't read your résumé.

It doesn't bow to your degrees.

It doesn't care that your mother preached from pulpits or that you can quote scripture and Freud in the same breath.

It sits anyway.

So I sat with it.

Studied the rhythm of my own pendulum.

Learned the architecture of my breakdowns.

Turned midnight moments into morning language.

This is not content.

This is soul work in stilettos — messy, beautiful, still standing.

This is cinematic healing in real time.

Bipolar disorder. Addiction. Recovery. Beauty. Grit.
Testimony.

The kind of truth you don't manufacture — or mass-
produce. You survive long enough to tell it.

Sedation is not peace.

Numb is not freedom.

Whiskey Prayers and Midnight Moments is what you write
when surviving is no longer enough.

It's what you build when perfection dies and direction takes
over.

Not halo.

Not highlight reel.

Nothing holy in the pretty way.

Just raw brilliance, still walking.

If you're looking for a sanitized redemption arc, this isn't it.

If you're here for confession with cadence — pull up a chair.

My voice is louder than the silence I once survived.

We're not whispering anymore

Author's Note

I didn't write this book to offer answers or diagnoses. I wrote it because there was a point in my life when language failed me — when clinical terms, labels, and explanations could no longer hold the weight of what I was surviving.

Therapy helped me understand.

Recovery helped me stabilize.

But soul work helped me remember who I was when my mind could no longer recognize me.

There are marks we don't choose—stories etched into us like a silent brand, passed down through systems, history, and expectation. For a long time, I carried my diagnosis the way generations before me carried imposed names and meanings: as something defining, limiting, and heavy. Education gave me insight. Lived experience gave me clarity. Soul work gave me my way back.

This book lives in the space where clinical language runs out and deeper knowing begins—where ancestry, intuition, ritual, grit, faith, and self-trust fill the gaps. It is not about perfection. It is about clarity. It is about surviving inside systems that were never built to hold us fully — and learning how to build something truer within ourselves.

My purpose is simple but urgent: to help make mental health conversations more honest, culturally aware, and universally accessible — without stripping them of depth, dignity, or humanity.

Table of Contents

The day I almost died, nobody noticed —

not even me.

This is not trauma porn.

This is testimony with grit.

That moment didn't look like chaos on the outside.

It looked like living.

But that was the day Whiskey Prayers and Midnight Moments was born —

born from ashes, without a name,

breathing quietly,

waiting for me to survive long enough

to tell the truth.

Chapter 1: Marked Not Finished

The Day Everything Changed

Everyone has a story.

Mine was whispered in midnight prayers and drowned in whiskey.

Not polished.

Not perfect.

Stitched together with blood and breath.

A masterpiece in progress — tempered, not broken.

This isn't background noise.

It's a siren you hear — warning you that strength doesn't always sound like silence, and survival doesn't always look pretty.

This isn't about brokenness.

It's about what rises after the world decides you're finished.

That wasn't always the story people saw when they looked at me.

Before any of that, everything about my life suggested momentum.

I was the first Black Homecoming Queen at my college, carrying a 3.4 GPA, preparing for the GMAT, and even interviewing with the Pentagon.

I had also been selected for a prestigious Women's Leadership Seminar, one of seventy-five young women nationwide believed to represent the next generation of leadership.

On paper, I was winning.

Behind the scenes, I was cracking.

I smiled for the world while quietly drowning in fear.

The pressure to succeed, to excel, to prove everyone right about me pressed into my chest until breathing felt optional.

The cracks started small. Missed a call here. Skipped a meal there. Stayed in my room longer than usual. Then it wasn't meals — it was days. Entire nights pacing. Heart racing. Mind spiraling.

I was unraveling, and I didn't have the language to explain it.

I started retreating — skipping classes, dodging friends, ignoring phone calls. My world shrank to the size of my dorm room, and even that felt too big some days.

I wasn't eating. I was losing weight so fast people whispered about drugs. But it wasn't that. I didn't even like cigarettes, yet I smoked just to feel numb.

I'd sit in my car in the rain and wonder if hitting a tree would feel better than living through another day like this.

My parents didn't know how bad it was—until I stopped answering their calls altogether.

And when they finally reached me, my mother said,

"If you don't come home, we're coming to get you."

I packed what little I could — numb, shaking, ashamed — and drove back to Atlanta. It hit me at twenty-two.

No warning. No manual. No safety net. Just a sterile room. A quiet voice.

A diagnosis.

Bipolar Disorder.

To be exact: Bipolar I — the kind with manic highs that masquerade as superpowers, until the crash collects its collateral.

They labeled me, but never told me what to do with the rage — honey-thick in the mouth, razor-clean in the cut.

At first, it felt like a death sentence, not a detour.

They didn't hand me healing. They handed me fire. Branded me with a name I didn't ask for. Not just a diagnosis—an inheritance.

No brochure.

No roadmap.

Just a barcode stamped across the soul.

A scarlet letter whispering behind every smile, staining every plan I thought I had.

It cracked my world wide open. I didn't just receive a label.

I started a war.

A war within.

A war with silence.

A war with the system.

This isn't trauma porn. This is testimony with grit. Mental illness isn't just a conversation.

It's a revolution.

When it came for me, it was quiet. No thunder. No lightning. Just a slow unraveling of the self I once knew. I felt everything and nothing at once. My mind became a battleground with no clear sides—only explosions.

Nobody warned me I'd grieve a version of myself that never had the chance to fully exist.

I didn't get high.

I got lost.

Lost in moods.

Lost in rooms where I smiled wide enough to hide the spiral. They called it a disorder. I called it survival.

I spent years trying to research my way out of the diagnosis — memorizing symptoms, decoding medical language, convincing myself the label didn't belong to me.

I was too smart.

Too strong.

Too aware.

None of that saved me from the crash. Mental illness has no type.

No income bracket.

No skin tone.

No warning label.

I wore ambition like armor. Even armor cracks. What was breaking wasn't just my mind. It was my identity. My sense of self as a Black woman taught to endure, not unravel.

Before I had language, I had instinct. Before diagnoses, I had questions no one knew how to answer. I went looking for understanding the only way I knew how—through research, education, books written in sterile tones that never once looked like me.

They gave me terminology, not meaning. Explanation, not instruction. Therapy spoke in textbooks. Medication spoke in dosages.

None of it spoke in me.

So I translated again—this time with my body, my lineage, my memory, my faith. What the system called treatment, I experienced as survival work.

Soul work became the labor of learning myself again when the old map stopped working. Prayer without performance. Research without permission. Listening inward when the world grew loud.

This was not weakness.

This was survival with intention.

Bruised —

But not broken.

Raw honey.

Sharp edges

What tasted like resilience was about to test the edges of
everything I thought I understood.

I told myself I was steady.

I didn't realize the barrel was already under strain.

Normal Is Overrated

What is normal anyway?

Normal sounds stable. Fixed.

Something that holds its shape over time.

But how does that apply to a human mind?

To sanity.

To survival.

Are we broken because our chemistry doesn't perform the way society expects it to?

I've lived inside that question for twenty-five years.

History misunderstands people while they're alive,

and romanticizes them once they're gone.

Minds once labeled unstable are later called genius.

So who decides where brilliance ends and instability begins?

Clinical manuals try.

Labels try.

Society tries.

None of them get the final word on who I am.

A diagnosis may describe symptoms — it does not define identity.

Stigma does more damage than chemistry ever could.

It reduces a whole human to a headline.

Everyone carries some measure of chaos.

The issue isn't having it.

The issue is knowing yourself well enough to meet it before it consumes you.

They called it crazy.

I started calling it capacity — a nervous system stretched by survival.

They called it reckless.

I recognized rebirth — a woman shedding her skin.

Crazy was never a diagnosis. It was shorthand. It was discomfort. It was what people say when complexity makes them uneasy.

Crazy was never the problem. Unprepared was. Life doesn't arrive as a drizzle. It arrives as tidal waves.

Sexy was never red lipstick. It was war paint. It was survival dressed in composure. It was ownership learning to stand upright in a storm.

Soul work became my internal compass.

It cooled my weather system. It steadied the tide. I am not my diagnosis. I am not less than. I am human first. Always.

And maybe that's the real question — Who decided "crazy" was the answer? Who decided normal was the goal?

Normal is overrated, baby.

Give me soul. Give me truth. Give me the kind of peace that tastes like warm cornbread and quiet joy.

✦ ✦ ✦

Chapter 2: When the Barrel Breaks

The diagnosis shattered my world, but the hope that followed refused to die.

All I had left was a glimmer of light — thin, stubborn, almost defiant.

And for the first time, I allowed myself to consider that maybe — just maybe — there was still a future with my name on it.

I never signed up to become the poster child for bipolar disorder.

Who would?

The stigma seeps through every crack in society. It shows up in silence — in awkward glances — in the way people pull away once they learn the label.

I thought bipolar was clinical. Neutral. Medical.

But in practice, it meant broken.

Unstable.

Dangerous.

Less than.

Stigma runs deep. It tangles itself around the way people look at you, talk to you, and decide who you are before you finish your sentence.

You show up in rooms but slowly stop showing up in yourself.

Mental health is not entertainment. It is lived experience. It is breath and burden and body. Human first. Always.

Case in point.

I sat in a doctor's office filling out forms when he casually asked, "Any history of mental illness?"

"I was diagnosed Bipolar I over ten years ago," I replied.

His eyes widened. The warmth drained from the room. It was as if the calm, composed woman sitting in front of him no longer aligned with the word I had just spoken.

A few minutes later, the nurse leaned in. "Does he want to refer you to psych?"

I nodded.

She blinked. "Really? I wouldn't have guessed."

Was that reassurance? Or disbelief?

Because in that moment, I wasn't a person. I was a chart. A diagnosis inked onto paper.

People think breakdown looks dramatic—tears, noise, spectacle. But sometimes it arrives quietly. In stillness. In a slow retreat from yourself.

I didn't realize the barrel had cracked until I was already leaking—emotionally, mentally, spiritually.

I was the strong one. The polished one. The woman with answers and a beat face. But the cracks had been forming quietly underneath.

The real mask was flawless.

What people saw: Strong. Happy. Fine.

What I survived daily: Exhausted. Hiding. Fighting for my life.

Mental illness isn't always visible. But invisibility does not make it unreal.

When the pressure built, I didn't explode outward.

I imploded.

People don't talk about internal implosions—about what it feels like to be high-functioning and hollow. About wearing a mask so long it grows heavy on your face.

My breakdown moved like fog.

It looked like laughter at dinner and tears in the bathroom.

Like sleeping twelve hours and still waking up tired.

Like smiling at people I loved while mentally checking out.

I held the storm. I carried the weight.

People saw charisma. Intelligence. Wit.

They didn't see the crash that followed.

Some days, even I couldn't tell where brilliance ended and breakdown began.

Silence can be deafening. After the appointments. After the medication adjustments. After the emergency passes. You're left with the echo.

And the echo gets loud.

I didn't trust my own peace. Every calm day felt suspicious— like chaos was crouched nearby waiting to prove I was foolish for believing I was safe.

You don't walk out of war without the war still whispering.

When the barrel finally broke, I had two choices:

Leak until I disappeared.

Or gather the shattered pieces and rebuild the container.

I chose to rebuild.

With therapy.

With grace.

With trembling hands and broken prayers.

I stitched myself back together.

And that choice—that stubborn refusal to vanish—was the beginning of living again.

But living again didn't look cinematic. It looked like brushing my hair. Answering one call. Making it through a morning without unraveling.

That's what beginning again looked like.

I still carried invisible bruises. I still flinched when people said, "You don't look bipolar," as if suffering wears a uniform.

But I kept showing up.

For myself.

For the version of me that once begged for relief.

For the woman in the mirror who was tired of surviving with her shoulders clenched and her story silenced.

Every time I said, "I'm still here," I was choosing life.

And that kind of living isn't performance.

It isn't spectacle.

It's sacred.

Wisdom doesn't rush.

It sips.

It burns just enough to wake you up.

Chapter 3: Sipping on Insight

There comes a point in the journey when silence stops protecting you and starts poisoning you — when ignorance is no longer bliss, but bondage.

For me, that shift happened when I stopped asking, "Why me?" and started whispering, "Teach me."

After the diagnosis, I didn't want sympathy. I wanted understanding. I wasn't looking for a savior — I needed strategy. Because the only thing more terrifying than being labeled "crazy" was not understanding what it meant.

So, I got to work.

Knowledge became my lifeline. I dove into research, memoirs, medical journals, survivor stories — anything that could illuminate the path ahead. I studied symptoms. I mapped patterns. I kept mood journals. I tracked triggers. I read clinical language with a highlighter in one hand and a prayer in the other.

But when I searched for stories that looked like mine — Black women navigating bipolar disorder with dignity and grit — I found silence.

No mirror. No map. No cultural reflection.

That silence was loud. It suggested this conversation wasn't meant for us. That suggestion reinforced shame.

In our community, we're taught to pray it away. To keep it private. To survive without complaint. But what happens when prayer meets neurochemistry? When strength begins to look like suffering in disguise? When the family doesn't have the tools?

At twenty-two, the diagnosis felt like a death sentence. Decades later, I understand it differently now. It wasn't the end. It was information.

And information is power.

Post-diagnosis, identity gets blurry. What's "you," and what's the illness? That question haunted me. It's one of the cruelest tricks this disorder plays — the slow erosion of self. But education gave me language. And language gave me clarity.

I learned the difference between a mood swing and a bad day. Between intuition and anxiety. Between who I am and what the storm does.

This work is exhausting. But it's liberating.

Because once you understand the rhythm of your mind, you stop twirling in the dark. You stop mistaking chaos for character. You stop letting other people define your sanity.

You begin writing your own manual.

Yes, there's still a dance — between brilliance and burnout, between highs and heaviness. But knowing the pattern is how I reclaim authority. Once you can name the storm, you can prepare for it.

So, I suited up.

Therapy became sacred. Church became grounding. Medication shifted from punishment to peace treaty — a quiet agreement with my brain that we both deserve to survive. I built routines. I protected my rest. I made space for God and science at the same table.

And when depression whispered, "You're too much. You'll never get better,"

I whispered back, "Watch me."

One of the most powerful lessons therapy taught me: fear paralyzes — honesty frees.

I had to unlearn the lie that emotions equal weakness. Sadness isn't sin. Anger isn't rebellion. Vulnerability isn't failure. Emotions are not evidence of fragility — they are evidence of humanity.

And when despair lingers too long — when heaviness settles deep in the chest — that's the signal.

Get help.

Call someone.

Break silence before it breaks you.

You are not broken.

You are learning.

This isn't the end of the storm.

It's the moment you learn to name it.

Grab life by the horns

or it will drag you by your stilettos.

Sanity isn't stillness — it's balance in motion.

Chapter 4: A Clear Mind at Dawn

Sanity is not silence.

It's restraint.

It isn't the absence of emotion —

it's mastery in the middle of it.

It's hearing your thoughts run wild and choosing not to chase them.

It's fear knocking and deciding not to open the door.

That's awareness.

Sanity isn't a spotless record or a polished public smile. It isn't eight hours of sleep and a life neatly arranged.

I've smiled through storms.

Fooled rooms full of people while my mind sprinted — thoughts unraveling faster than I could catch them.

Sanity, for me, is not perfection.

It's interception.

It's recognizing the shift before the spiral.

I've lived through chemical roulette.

Mid-manic — heart racing, invincible, rewriting my future at midnight. Certain I could rebuild Rome before sunrise.

Then the crash.

Heavy. Dark. Hollow.

Not sadness — burial.

The roller coaster doesn't glide. It slams. It flips without warning. No seatbelt. No script.

Healing began when I stopped ignoring the signals.

Missed meals. Restless nights. Thoughts that wouldn't slow down.

Instead of fighting them, I listened.

That internal voice I once dismissed began whispering truth:

You can't live in the eye of the storm and still expect to feel safe.

So, I adjusted.

I anchored myself in routine. In therapy. In check-ins. In small, quiet stabilizers — water, breath, prayer, rest.

I learned I am not helpless. I am not at the mercy of a label.

I have power.

The power to intercept. To pivot. To pause. To rest.

That's what a clear mind looks like now.

Not flawless.

But aware.

Dawn doesn't offer comfort.

Dawn tests resolve.

And every morning, I answer —

steady-handed, clear-eyed,

balance over collapse.

That's the work.

Not glamorous.

Necessary.

People think healing is loud. It's not.

Healing is choosing yourself again after the fire.

Not perfection. Not applause.

Just staying - breath by breath.

"I'm still here. And that's the win."

Healing isn't loud. It's intentional.

Chapter 5: Raw Honey and Sharp Edges

They called it a diagnosis.

I called it a detour with blades.

No one told me what to do with the quiet wounds — the ones that don't bleed but burn. The ones hidden beneath perfectly contoured cheeks and cherry-red lips. Mental illness isn't always loud. Sometimes it's silence with teeth.

There was no smooth path forward. Just jagged mornings. Medicated nights. Realizations that stung like alcohol poured over open skin.

I wasn't healed.

I was hardened.

Reshaped by fire — not therapy brochures.

The girl in the mirror wore lipstick, yes. But the gloss was war paint. Behind the shine was exhaustion. Behind the exhaustion was survival — sealed tight with concealer and a half-smile.

I didn't break all at once. It was a slow unraveling.

Some days were sweet as raw honey.

Other days were jagged as broken glass.

I showed up for people who didn't know I was drowning. My journals became proof that I still existed beyond the label. Nobody knew how many nights I cried into the same pillow I had fluffed to perfection that morning.

Some days I drank my silence like communion.

Some nights I screamed without sound.

And somewhere in between, I stopped talking.

Not for an hour. Not for a day. For months.

Depression folded my voice into itself. My mother carried me into a hospital because I had gone catatonic — and let me be clear: I have never been a quiet woman. That wasn't peace.

That was prison.

There were seasons where I couldn't eat. Couldn't move. Couldn't answer the phone. My brother told people I was asleep or out of town.

The truth?

I was in a quiet hell.

The kind of silence that convinces you you're already dead while you're still breathing.

Winter meant relapse.

Summer meant rebirth.

I lived in that cycle for years — working part-time because my body could not survive the cold months. I lost time. I lost people. I almost lost myself.

Mania didn't look glamorous.

It looked like three days awake.

Fast-talking brilliance dressed up as destiny.

Grand plans at midnight.

Walking into rooms like I owned them while my life quietly caught fire behind me.

And then the crash.

The fire turned to smoke.

The sparkle turned to silence.

The pendulum didn't just swing — it hijacked everything.

That's the part people don't understand.

They think mania is energy.

They don't see the wreckage.

Healing didn't arrive like a flood.

It came in drops.

Cold. Reluctant. Sharp.

There were days I couldn't even open my front door. I would sit on the patio, staring at the sunlight, willing myself to just… move.

That was the battlefield.

That was paralysis.

I didn't wake up and decide to heal.

I clawed my way back.

I researched my mind like it was a case study. I made playlists.
I journaled. I turned my living room into a one-woman psych
lab. I did light therapy. I prayed whiskey-soaked prayers at
3:17 a.m. and made promises to myself with shaking hands.

And somewhere in all that grit, I learned something new.

I didn't learn this in a seminar.

I built it in survival.

I call it the trifecta of healing: raw reflections, inner truth, and
self-discovery.

Raw reflection forces you to see what happened without
romance.

Inner truth demands you name what hurt without shrinking
it.

Self-discovery asks who you are beyond the wound.

That became my framework. My anchor. My return point.

Don't let your diagnosis drive your life.

Get in the damn driver's seat.

So I built a toolbox.

Breathing techniques.

Routine.

Boundaries.

Faith.

Science.

Grace.

Stretching through stigma.

Learning when to sit still and when to fight.

Tending wounds with language — writing as sutures.

You wouldn't have seen it looking at me then — how jagged it was inside. How many broken truths I swallowed just to survive tomorrow.

But I carried it.

Quietly.

Beautifully.

With edges still sharp enough to cut.

I wasn't soft anymore.

I was raw honey distilled by pain. Sweet enough to survive. Sharp enough to protect.

I wasn't just living with a diagnosis.

I was living beyond it.

Every meltdown I survived was rebellion.

Every morning I showed up was protest.

Every day I didn't give up — prayer.

Healing isn't spa days and scented candles.

Sometimes healing is rage.

Sometimes it is risk.

Most days it is raw honey and sharp edges.

Some days I glam up.

Some days I can barely rise.

But don't get it twisted.

The gloss isn't vanity.

It's armor.

There's a kind of freedom in daring to dream again after a diagnosis.

A diagnosis can shrink the future. Make ambition feel dangerous. Make hope feel irresponsible.

Healing widens it back.

There is power in planning for years you once weren't sure you would survive. There is strength in setting goals when you once set alarms just to make it through the night.

Dreaming again is not delusion.

It's proof that survival was never the finish line.

And sometimes I still sit on the patio, not for the sun, but to remember that I opened the door.

I moved. I didn't stop.

I'm not just surviving.

I'm sharpening.

Red bottoms don't shield me from antagonism.

Stilettos don't soften stigma.

Designer heels don't rewrite a diagnosis.

I'm human first.

Chapter 6: Cheesecake and Stilettos

Survival Taught Me Timing

Life is a trapeze act, even in red bottoms.

It's rhythm and risk. You learn when to vault and when to hold the bar. The fall isn't the lesson. The timing is.

Survival reshaped me.

Not into someone softer.

Not into someone silent.

But into someone strategic.

Life lessons are threads in the tapestry I'm still becoming. Every scar adds depth. Every misstep adds color. Nothing here was wasted — not the breakdown, not the silence, not the sharp edges.

After the burn of raw honey came something else.

Precision.

My peace didn't get quieter — it got louder, clearer, less interested in proving, and more invested in protecting.

I didn't disappear. I refined.

Survival taught me momentum over fear — no matter the season, no matter the terrain. Life keeps moving whether you're steady or spiraling. The work is learning how to move with it.

The real discipline is knowing what is you — and what is the illness.

Knowing when a thought is fear. Knowing when a mood is chemistry. Knowing when silence is reflection—and when it is avoidance dressed up as maturity.

That awareness changes everything.

Because living with mental illness is already complex. Add stigma. Add expectation. Add substance use. Add the secrets you were taught not to say out loud. Leave them unspoken long enough, and they don't disappear. They calcify. They surface sideways. They start steering your life.

And that's when timing matters.

Life isn't just cheesecake and stilettos — sweet indulgence and polished confidence. It's pressure under heels. It's learning how to walk steadily when the ground shifts.

I used to think stillness meant safety.

Now I know better.

Sometimes stillness is fear sitting quietly, pretending to be peace.

Survival taught me how to tell the difference.

It taught me how to regulate before I erupt.

How to move before I sink.

How to check myself before chaos checks me.

It taught me timing.

Because life plays games whether you're ready or not. The Jedi mind tricks. The curve balls. The detours with blades. And if you don't learn when to pivot, you get dragged —

dragged where I once was, by my own damn stilettos.

So I adjusted.

Not perfectly. Not flawlessly. But intentionally.

I stopped waiting for ideal conditions. I stopped demanding certainty before movement. I stopped mistaking paralysis for patience.

Fear had its moment.

But I kept mine.

Lipstick on Shattered Glass

The lipstick wasn't just color.

It was armor.

A quiet rebellion painted red. No one wants the woman behind the glass — they want her polished, powdered, posed.

Pretty. Presentable. Palatable.

So she obliged.

Swipe.

Gloss.

Smile.

The mirror simmered with lies. It told her she was too bold.

Too loud.

Too Black.

Too broken.

Too much.

So she became all of it. Behind the shimmer was survival.

Behind the lashes was exhaustion. Behind the red was rage she didn't know where to put.

She didn't fall apart quietly. She shattered. And somewhere between the crack in the glass and the crack in her voice, she realized — the mirror didn't lie. She did.

She told herself she wasn't worth saving.

Lipstick on shattered glass looks beautiful from far away.

Up close, you can see where it split.

Chapter 7: She Wore Lipstick Too

Some women wear lipstick for beauty.

I wore mine for battle.

I painted my lips like armor — lined in defiance, filled in with silence. Ruby red. Deep wine. Anything bold enough to cover the scream I didn't know how to let out. This wasn't glam.

This was camouflage.

After the diagnosis, I didn't disappear.

I performed.

Flawless skin. Perfect lashes. Concealer thick enough to hide how hollow I felt.

I wasn't ready to be seen without polish. I wasn't ready to admit I didn't recognize myself in the mirror.

Because the mirror lied.

Or at least that's what I told myself.

It showed me a ghost wearing my face. It whispered that I was only what I had lost. Only the label they said behind my back.

Bipolar.

Marked.

Branded.

I hid behind everything I was raised to be—not the values, but the image of it. Educated. Polished. Strong Black family. Middle class. High-achieving. Untouchable.

But inside, I felt like damaged goods.

And in our community, there is no margin for "crazy."

You don't cry mental illness in a world that already doubts your competence. You don't unravel publicly when strength is your inheritance.

So I masked it.

I distanced myself from family. From successful friends. From anyone who reminded me of who I used to be.

I didn't want their questions.

I didn't want their hope.

I didn't want the expectation that I would rise.

I didn't feel I deserved to.

I didn't grow up wanting to be the poster child for bipolar. I wanted to be a success story.

Instead, I went from promise to

punchline overnight.

The pendulum didn't just swing.

It crashed.

Manic highs that made me feel unstoppable. Depressive lows that buried me alive. Gloss on the surface. Grief underneath.

Once, a friend told me she needed distance. She was pregnant — newly professional, newly settled — and said she had to protect her peace. I understood the words, but I heard what wasn't said. My diagnosis made me unpredictable in her world. Inconvenient. Too unstable for a life that was carefully aligning itself toward promotions and nurseries and polished futures. I had once been the overachiever at the table. Now I was the cautionary tale with perfect lashes.

There was stigma within my friend groups, but it didn't always come dressed as cruelty. It was confusion. We were young. Mental health wasn't language we'd been trained to hold. Some of them tried. Some asked careful questions. But understanding requires stamina. And at twenty-two, most of us were still learning how to manage our own storms. Life kept moving. They built careers and families. I fought to stabilize myself. We drifted — not out of hatred, but out of limitation.

I stopped trying to measure my life against theirs. What they achieved. What I achieved. What came easier for them. Comparison becomes poison when your nervous system is already at war. My life took a different route. Not lesser. Just harder in places most people never see.

Because when you live with a diagnosis, showing up is not casual. It is deliberate. Some days the win is not ambition. It is getting out of bed. Medication may steady chemistry. It does not erase effort. There is always that quiet internal negotiation — get up, breathe, move, try again tomorrow. That is maintenance. And maintenance is strength.

They saw the lipstick.

Nobody saw the fracture.

And the longer I performed, the more exhausted I became. Because pretending is heavier than pain.

Eventually, the mask began to peel.

Because stigma doesn't just isolate you.

It exhausts you.

It convinces you that silence is strength and performance is protection.

But silence nearly swallowed me whole.

So I had to learn the difference between presentation and identity.

Between survival and self-erasure.

Healing didn't begin when I removed the lipstick.

It began when I stopped needing it to feel worthy.

She wore lipstick too.

And still made it.

I didn't want sobriety.

I wanted better excuses.

I didn't call it addiction.

I called it timing.

I'd stop once the program started.

That was the deal I made with myself.

The lie wasn't convincing anymore.

No label needed.

Chapter 8: The Battle Within

If lipstick was my armor, alcohol was my anesthesia.

And that damn bottle?

That was a different kind of war.

The battle within doesn't happen in the streets. It happens in silence — in the space between diagnosis and denial, in the hour between rage and relapse. This was my war. The kind you don't train for. The kind you survive on instinct, grit — and sometimes by accident.

I didn't grow up expecting to be the poster child for bipolar disorder. I didn't dream of writing about addiction or prison. I dreamed of being someone. The first to make it big. The polished one. The success story.

And I was — until I wasn't.

Until the diagnosis detonated everything I thought I knew about myself.

Until alcohol became my escape and shame my second skin.

I've been through more than I ever expected to carry.

Highs that made me feel invincible. Lows that made me question whether I belonged here at all.

Over time, my diagnoses multiplied — Bipolar I, Anxiety, PTSD, Alcohol Use Disorder. Imagine sitting down every day to a mental table set with all of that and being expected to function like nothing is happening.

Mental health doesn't care about your resume, your income bracket, your zip code, or your family name. It doesn't discriminate based on dignity or degree. It simply arrives — and if you don't understand it, it will run your life.

The Invisible Wall

There was a battle inside the battle.

Not the loud one. Not the spiraling one.

The quiet one.

The one that happened in exam rooms.

When I was first diagnosed, my family and I were educated, accomplished, capable people. But we were unprepared. Mental illness wasn't a dinner-table discussion. It wasn't forbidden. It just wasn't something we had seen up close. And when it arrived, it didn't knock politely. It moved in.

We learned in real time.

I remember asking for a Black doctor. I didn't want what I thought was someone else's narrative placed on me. I wanted someone who understood the cultural weight of the word bipolar in a conservative Black household. I wanted to feel seen.

She told me something I didn't want to hear:

"If you don't take medication, you won't accomplish what you say you want to accomplish."

At the time, it felt extreme.

Looking back, there was truth in it.

Medication is not for everybody. But for me, it became part of the journey. Not immediately. Not easily. And not without cost.

The trial years felt less like treatment and more like experimentation. I was handed one prescription, then another. Doses adjusted. Side effects monitored. I felt like a lab rat at times — a body reacting to chemical guesses. Some medications flattened me. Some pushed me toward mania. Some made my thoughts feel foreign inside my own skull.

And then there was my body.

One medication came with the risk of weight gain. It delivered on that promise. I watched myself expand physically while feeling like I was shrinking internally. My body shifted in ways I wasn't prepared for. No one tells you stabilizing the mind can challenge the body. No one talks about that part.

The physical cost became serious enough that I had to make difficult medical decisions to restore balance to my body. That chapter was private. It was humbling. It was not cosmetic. It was survival of a different kind.

No one tells you the invisible wall you hit when you're trying to do everything "right" and still paying in other ways.

For years, I was rigid. Denial can feel like strength when you don't know what else to hold onto. I resisted the diagnosis. It took nearly five years before I fully accepted that this wasn't a temporary interruption — it was something I would have to learn to live with.

Understanding did not come all at once. It came slowly. Through research. Through tears. Through uncomfortable conversations. Through side effects.

Eventually, I stopped being passive in the process.

If a medication didn't feel right, I said so.

If a side effect was unbearable, I spoke up.

If something didn't align with my body or mind, I refused it.

I learned that managing mental health is not surrendering control. It is participating in your own care.

Everybody metabolizes medicine differently. Everybody carries risk differently. You have to pay attention. You have to advocate. You have to know your own warning signs — not just emotionally, but physically.

That was the invisible wall — no applause, no poetry, just the slow shift from survival to responsibility.

Mental health was not a conversation in my community. Managing my illness was one thing. Speaking about it was another.

So, I learned to find humor where I could. Laughter became medicine. Music became therapy. If I didn't laugh, I felt abnormal — like some strange, fractured version of myself.

But underneath the humor was a harder question:

Who was I before all of this?

Before the diagnosis. Before the stigma. Before the chaos. Before I learned how to shrink and stretch depending on who was watching.

What was my original canvas?

Was I still a masterpiece? Or had life edited me down to a survival sketch?

That question changed everything.

Because the journey back to your original canvas isn't about becoming someone new.

It's about remembering who you were before the world layered noise over your truth.

There is no pity for the one drowning in alcohol.

People think you choose it.

But if I had been hooked on crack, maybe someone would have shown sympathy.

The bottle nearly buried me – but I survived it.

That damn bottle followed me everywhere – not in my hands anymore, but in memory. And memory is louder than any liquor store door.

I was once chained to the ritual of drinking — enslaved to it as a means of coping. I knew every liquor store. Every closing time. Every loophole. Every justification. I didn't just drink. I engineered access to it.

I've had slips.

I won't romanticize that.

But I won't erase the truth either.

Today I walk past it not because I forgot —

I walk past it because I remember too well.

I remember rock bottom.

I remember the chain reaction it unleashed.

I remember how fast dignity evaporates when the bottle becomes the negotiator.

But the truth is, it didn't start that way.

The bottle didn't arrive overnight. It crept in, dressed like control. Social sips turned into survival swallows. Wine on a Wednesday became brown-bag mornings and 3 a.m. confessions whispered into the steering wheel. Addiction doesn't kick down the door. It slides in through the cracks.

Eventually it stopped being a celebration and became a ritual — a rhythm of self-destruction I could perform in my sleep.

Eventually, I found myself making hour-and-fifteen-minute drives to Atlanta under the lie of love. Saying I was dating someone. That was partially true. But the real romance was between me and the high. Cocaine. Alcohol. Hotel rooms I didn't book for rest but for refuge — from myself.

I'd party while they were at work, clean up just enough by the time they got home to seem functional. That was the cover story. Eventually, even that became exhausting. So I brought the supply home. Had it delivered to my doorstep. Atlanta to my front door — no questions asked.

One night, I was one exit away from home when I saw the blue lights. I was drunk. I had cocaine in my pocket. I refused the breathalyzer. I don't even remember the test. The report said I was swerving all over the highway.

I could've killed someone.

I thank God I didn't.

That DUI may have saved my life — and someone else's.

I went to jail. Twenty days.

I read the police report over and over, crying. Not because I was innocent. But because I wasn't. I had become someone I couldn't even recognize.

My license was gone. My car impounded. My reputation shattered. Rehab was court-ordered. This time, I couldn't fake my way out. I had to show up or go to prison.

And still — I drank.

I thought I could outsmart the system. I tracked my drug tests. I drank on off days. I tried to be strategic with the hangovers. I was juggling a lie with no safety net.

My mother called me after I got home from jail and asked, "Are you in the sauce again?"

She wasn't angry. She was exhausted.

My parents had been my anchors, but I had cut every rope. I thought I was too clever to be caught, too charming to be punished.

But grace was running out.

I failed my rehab drug tests. Lost my first offender's program. I was sentenced to two months in prison.

Prison was a wake-up call with cold floors and metal echoes. No gloss. No filter. Just a broken woman in county orange wondering how the hell she ended up there.

All this… over that damn bottle.

People don't pity the alcoholic like they do other addictions. It's sold in stores. Wrapped in class and celebration. Nobody sees the blood on the cork. Nobody sees the woman unraveling behind the wine glass.

But I was dying.

Quietly. Elegantly. Destroying my body in high heels and silence.

Sobriety wasn't the punishment. It was the rescue I kept running from.

Every drink was a love letter to my own destruction, sealed with shame and swallowed in silence. I hadn't hit bottom because I didn't believe there was one. I thought the fall was endless. I thought I'd float forever.

But I crashed.

Being dually diagnosed with bipolar disorder and alcoholism felt like living in a house with no door. I kept falling through. PTSD and anxiety hung overhead — fragile and always threatening to shatter.

There were nights I swallowed pills with prayer. Days I drank my pain like water. Not because I wanted to die. But because I didn't want to feel.

The in-between was the killer — the place between numb and breakdown. The part nobody prepares you for — the place where silence grows teeth.

Medication became a gamble.

Some days it saved me.

Other days it sedated me into oblivion.

Crawling on floors. Leaning on furniture just to stand up.

I couldn't eat.

Couldn't write.

Couldn't feel.

But I survived.

And survival meant building a toolbox. I journaled. I prayed. I showed up to therapy. I tracked triggers. I listened for God in the static.

The Impact Radius

The journey was never light. There were detours — and some of them were brutal.

It took years just to understand the diagnosis, years to soften enough to consider medication, years to move from rigidity to openness. I had to educate myself. I had to sit in therapy. I had to confront what I didn't want to believe.

And my family learned in real time.

Mental illness doesn't just visit the individual. It moves through the whole house.

People talk about addiction and programs like Al-Anon. They talk about the family learning to cope with alcoholism. But they don't speak enough about what happens when someone you love cycles through manic highs and crushing lows. What it does to a mother. To a sibling. To a child. To a friend.

The hospitalizations.

The assessments.

The sterile intake questions.

The waiting.

When you call 911 and say you're not okay, there's a sequence that begins. You are picked up. You are evaluated. You are placed somewhere. Sometimes it's the right place. Sometimes it's simply the available place.

Your loved ones stand outside that process with limited control. They witness the swings. They absorb the fear. They learn the protocols by necessity, not choice.

And over time, they build endurance too.

I learned something crucial: support systems are not optional. They are structural.

When my mind could not regulate itself, someone else steadied the room. When I could not see clearly, someone reminded me who I was. Not perfectly. Not always. But consistently enough to matter.

Recovery is not only an addiction word. It is a mental health word. It is what happens when you fight to return to yourself. When you relearn how to enjoy what you once loved. When you rebuild daily rhythm. When you practice coping like a skill — not a personality trait.

It can feel like learning to walk again.

And the ones who love you? They learn to walk alongside you.

Eventually, I stopped letting the diagnosis write my story.

I picked up my own damn pen.

I wasn't lazy. I wasn't broken.

I was diagnosed.

And still — I showed up.

I was a functioning entrepreneur with a disorder. Balancing brilliance and breakdown. And when I was stable — I shined.

Seasonal depression hit like a thief. Six months of light. Six months of shadow. I wasn't a failure. I was cycling. I wasn't incapable. I was managing.

Even in my madness, I kept going.

I'm not my label. I'm not my lowest moment. I'm not that damn bottle.

I am a woman still defining what success looks like in my own skin.

Stability was not handed to me.

It was negotiated.

Monitored.

Defended.

Maintained.

That is the battle no one sees.

This mind — flawed, brilliant, regulated or raw —

is still mine to lead from.

I stopped surviving. I started thriving.

And that was the real battle won.

Chapter 9: The Velvet Rage & Diamond Heart

There's a kind of silence that masquerades as strength.

It dresses in velvet.

Walks in heels through hell.

Clutches rage like pearls.

Not loud rage.

Not door-slamming rage.

The kind that sets the table, sends emails, remembers the birthday — while quietly cracking underneath.

I was in my forties by then.

Grown. Educated. Fully aware of what life costs.

And still vibrating under the surface like a power line no one could see humming.

They said I was composed.

Graceful.

Holding it together.

What they didn't know?

I wasn't holding it together.

I was holding everything.

That's velvet rage.

It doesn't explode. It curates.

It camouflages breakdown in discipline.

It performs healing while still bleeding backstage.

I looked healed.

Sounded healed.

Moved like I was good.

But inside? The machine was still running.

The rage machine.

Full speed.

I wasn't angry at the world.

I was angry at myself.

For the time I lost.

For the lies I told.

For how long I believed I was too far gone to be restored.

I had diagnoses stacked on the table like a cocktail menu — bipolar, PTSD, anxiety, alcoholism. Imagine waking up each day and swallowing that before breakfast.

And still smiling at brunch.

That's velvet rage.

It's mascara that doesn't smudge because the tears dried before they fell.

It's hosting dinner while your chest feels like it's caving in.

It's answering "I'm fine" so many times you almost believe it.

Strength became a costume.

Not by choice — by expectation.

In the Black community, you don't unravel loudly.

You endure.

You perform resilience.

So I did.

I wore my rage in red lipstick.

In controlled tones.

In politeness that concealed panic.

But healing doesn't come from performance.

It comes from fracture.

And one night — after the breakdowns, after the jail, after that damn bottle — something inside me shifted.

Not dramatic.

Not cinematic.

Just a whisper:

Not like this.

I didn't roar when I raged. I simmered. Velvet rage wrapped me in tension — soft enough to breathe, sharp enough to cut shame out by the root.

I got tired of performing survival, tired of shrinking my feelings into something digestible, tired of curating pain so it wouldn't make others uncomfortable.

Underneath the rage, there was something else — pressure. And under pressure, diamond forms.

A diamond heart isn't cute. It isn't soft. It's forged — built in silence, pressed under expectation, refined by breakdown.

It doesn't sparkle for applause. It shines because it survived. Velvet rage gave me fire. Diamond heart gave me form.

Now when people say bipolar like it's a slur, I don't flinch. I've lived through mania that felt electric, depression that felt like drowning without water, addiction that drifted like smoke through my lungs. Velvet rage isn't chaos. It's control — heat restrained with memory, softness that learned how to survive steel.

For a long time, I tried to make my power small — quieter, easier to digest. I thought maybe if I rounded my edges, the world would feel less threatened by me. But shrinking never built anything worth standing in.

Let them chase average.

I was born with fire in my bones and blueprints in my bloodstream. I bend rules like velvet over steel. I break silence like glass under bourbon. I build what they said couldn't exist — woman, whole, unapologetic.

That's not arrogance. That's architecture. That's what happens when pain turns into precision and survival turns into design. Velvet rage isn't destruction. It's discipline. The anger didn't disappear — it sharpened. I learned restraint. I learned aim. Diamond heart measured heat. Power without performance.

The trials didn't break me — they forged me.

Peace didn't find me. I built it.

I am not reborn. I'm reoriented.

A new posture. A new pulse. A new calibration of power.

I know the dance now.

I learned the language of the tango stitched through my lived truth.

I move in step with my becoming.

I know the storm, but I also know the center. Knowledge became power. Education became strategy. Therapy became sacred. Rest became rebellion. I'm no longer afraid of the pendulum. I track it. I steady it. I face it when it growls. Not perfectly — consciously. That was the shift.

Not cured — clear.

Not flawless — forged.

Not reinvented — reclaimed.

My healing wasn't linear.

It wasn't pretty.

It wasn't Instagrammable.

It was crawling through shattered glass and calling it progress.

It was waking up with grit in my teeth and choosing to stand anyway.

It was studying my own triggers like blueprints.

It was losing my mind — and rebuilding it with tools I forged
in the wreckage.

I didn't glow up.

I clawed up.

I am not the woman who broke.

I am the woman who swallowed dust.

Who bled without applause.

Who learned to visit her own chaos

and now dances in the storm instead of running from it.

Some days I don't know if I'm outrunning my old self

or chasing the woman I'm becoming.

Am I running from her — or toward me?

The past still knows my weak spots.

It still remembers how I used to fold.

But the future?

She demands velocity.

And I am no longer built to crawl.

This isn't damage.

This is discipline.

This is ownership.

This is becoming.

Healing didn't erase the rage.

It taught me how to carry it without being consumed by it.

This is what it means to hold yourself together long enough to rebuild.

This is velvet.

This is diamond.

This is a grown woman healing.

And just when I thought I had mastered composure, the next lesson waited. Even diamonds crack under the wrong pressure.

These are the reflections that surface

after chaos drains itself.

After the barrel breaks.

After the noise exhausts its own echo

In the quiet, I don't panic.

I breathe resilience.

I let stillness rebuild me.

Silence is not absence.

It's recovery.

Chapter 10: The Art of Falling Apart

Falling apart isn't always loud.

Sometimes it hums like a broken lullaby in the back of your throat.

Sometimes it's pearls, lashes, posture —

a smile so fixed it could crack under the weight of your own truth.

Ever look in the mirror and not recognize the woman staring back?

That was me.

Midlife.

Grown.

Educated.

Still spiraling.

The fall didn't come with sirens.

It showed up in sips.

In secrets.

That damn bottle sat quiet like it wasn't orchestrating my life.

And it wasn't just the diagnosis.

Bipolar.

Anxiety.

Trauma.

And that damn bottle —

waiting in the wings, amplifying everything it touched and daring me to believe I was still in control.

It didn't arrive alone.

It partnered with the pendulum.

It fed the silence.

It complicated the fall.

And that's how it began.

The night my hair was laid.

Makeup blended.

Outfit intentional.

I knew how to look safe.

Blue lights washed over fresh edges and glossed lips.

"Ma'am, have you been drinking?"

My breath answered before I did.

They asked for the breathalyzer.

That little machine.

That little tube.

That little mirror you can't negotiate with.

I refused.

Not loud.

Not dramatic.

Just steady.

Like I still had power.

Like I could outsmart numbers.

Like grown women in their forties don't get reduced to decimals on asphalt.

But breath doesn't lie.

Breath carries everything you tried to perfume.

The air between me and that officer felt thick.

Cement heavy.

Final.

Funny how your lungs betray you before your mouth ever does.

He nodded like the decision was already made.

The cuffs weren't violent.

But that click?

That click sounded permanent.

The ride was quiet.

No screaming.

No collapse.

Just mascara.

Metal.

Denial sat in my lap like a purse I didn't want to claim.

Concrete floors don't care about your lifestyle.

Cement walls don't care about degrees.

County orange doesn't care you were polished last week.

Confinement starts long before the cell door closes.

I wish I could tell you that night was the turning point.

It wasn't.

I was thinking about my next drink before I signed release papers.

That's the part people don't say out loud.

Addiction doesn't always humble you immediately.

Sometimes it just embarrasses you.

I went home and put my face back on.

Voice calm.

Hair done.

Story ready.

"I'm fine."

I told myself I'd stop once the program started.

Until then, I drank.

I thought I could game the system — track tests, drink around rules, breathe clean when it mattered.

But the air remembers.

And that damn bottle was no longer a habit.

It was a lifestyle.

You don't drink to feel good forever.

At some point you drink to feel nothing.

And nothing starts to feel like relief.

Depression came in waves — grief some days, numbness others.

Mania followed like electricity through exposed wiring.

I could write business plans at 3 a.m. and unravel 24 hours later.

This was the pendulum.

Midlife and still swinging.

I wasn't weak.

I wasn't stupid.

I was exhausted.

Exhausted from performing strength.

Exhausted from looking polished while unraveling internally.

Exhausted from proving I wasn't broken while clearly cracking.

There is an elegance to how pain performs.

Lipstick.

Calendar invites.

Dinner plans.

And then silence, so loud it hums in your teeth.

Therapy eventually made me sit still long enough to listen.

To the negative self-talk.

To the inherited fear.

To the shame.

I had to challenge the script running in my head.

I had to relearn how to breathe without poisoning myself.

That's the alchemy nobody talks about.

Falling apart doesn't mean you're done.

Sometimes it means you're shedding a version of yourself that could no longer carry you.

I forgave the version of me who didn't know better.

I forgave the version who did — and still reached for chaos.

And I built a bridge between them.

Brick by breath.

Truth by truth.

Falling apart wasn't the shame.

Staying there would have been.

I didn't collapse.

I cracked open.

And somewhere between cement floors and whispered prayers, I started choosing differently.

Not perfectly.

Differently.

That's the art of it.

The art of falling apart isn't destruction.

It's revelation.

Recovery Is Not an Aesthetic

The bottle is no longer my escape.

Not my solution.

Not the center of my mental space.

Sobriety didn't give me perfection.

It gave me my life back.

And that is not a small thing.

I didn't grow up wanting to be the poster child for recovery.

But I refuse to stay silent about what almost killed me.

Recovery isn't aesthetic.

It isn't a vibe.

It isn't a hashtag.

It is moment-by-moment honesty that demands self-awareness, spirituality, and courage every single day.

You don't get to lie to yourself and survive.

You face yourself — because your life depends on it.

Some days the mirror lies.

Recovery demands truth anyway.

No more dry drunk — sober in body, still enslaved in mind.

No more pretending.

This is recovery with a pulse.

Not polished.

Not packaged.

Alive.

✦ ✦ ✦

Chapter 11: Lipstick or Addiction

There's a fine line between a beat face and a broken soul.

Lipstick or addiction — sometimes you can't tell the difference.

Addiction doesn't always show up in back alleys and dirty mirrors.

Sometimes it shows up in red lipstick, strong brows, pressed hair, and perfectly controlled posture.

Sometimes it looks polished.

Composed.

Successful.

The glam was never just glam.

It was armor.

Because when you don't know how to heal, you learn how to hide.

I didn't grow up fearing addiction. I thought it was sophisticated. Cigarettes. Cocktails. Status. That grown energy.

I never imagined it would become the thing that threatened everything.

Alcohol became the silent partner to my diagnosis.

Bipolar was the imbalance.

The bottle was the accelerate.

They worked together more than I wanted to admit.

I didn't even enjoy drinking socially. I preferred isolation. The bottle became a therapist, a confidant, a distraction. It took the edge off mania. It softened depression. It blurred shame.

But blurred is not healed.

Eventually I had to ask myself the question that split me open.

When I look at shattered glass in the mirror —

lipstick smeared like war paint sliding off a tired face…

or a whiskey glass rimmed with the ghost of last night's pour —

I don't see glamour.

I see fracture.

I ask myself, quietly but honestly:

Would I rather wear lipstick on my face

or whiskey on my breath?

Both were costumes.

Both were survival tactics.

I took the keys at the edge of hell and said no.

Recovery isn't aesthetic. It's real as hell.

The cravings don't knock.

They slide in. Midnight smooth.

Like they helped pay rent on my pain.

That damn bottle knew my diagnosis by name.

Sat beside my bipolar.

Waited for the crash.

Volunteered as comfort when the pendulum swung too far.

It didn't save me.

It sedated me.

And sedation isn't peace.

I hit my knees —

not because I was holy.

Not because I had a polished prayer life.

Not because I suddenly got sanctified in the middle of my mess.

Not because the ceiling opened and angels started harmonizing over my downfall.

I hit my knees because I was tired.

Tired of pretending I had control.

Tired of negotiating with that damn bottle like it was a business partner.

Tired of saying "just one more" like that hadn't been the lie for ten years.

I wasn't holy.

I was hemorrhaging.

I wasn't kneeling out of reverence.

I was collapsing under the weight of my own illusions.

There's a difference.

Holiness is aspiration.

Exhaustion is surrender.

And mine was surrender.

I wasn't quoting scripture.

I was whispering survival.

Rebirth me.

Not because I deserve it —

because I can't keep living like this.

Strip the performance.

Rip off the glamour.

Burn the fake control I wrapped around my chaos.

I didn't want applause.

I wanted relief.

That's when the shift began.

Not in perfection.

Not in some cleaned-up testimonial.

But in raw, midlife, mascara-running, grown-woman truth.

And maybe that's more sacred than holy.

Because that's where direction is born.

When you stop asking to look righteous

and start asking to be real.

That moment wasn't a miracle.

It was a pivot.

Breaking My Own Chains

The day I stopped drinking wasn't cinematic.

There was no triumphant music. No tearful confession. No dramatic pour down the sink.

It was quiet.

Which is somehow more terrifying.

Because quiet means no audience. No applause. No one clapping for your decision to live.

I stopped when drinking stopped being indulgence and became inheritance.

Not inheritance from family — inheritance from pain.

It had moved from habit to hunger. From hunger to dependence. From dependence to survival.

And survival shouldn't taste like anesthesia.

I remember waking up with my heart racing before my eyes even opened. That hollow fear. That crawling dread. The negotiation began before my feet hit the floor.

Maybe just one to steady myself.

That's when I knew it wasn't casual anymore.

It was chemical.

Alcohol wasn't a glass. It was a leash.

It wasn't celebration. It was sedation.

And sedation only delays the collapse.

I had seen the soul of that bottle.

It was empty.

And it wanted me empty too.

People ask why someone stops drinking like they're asking why someone changes their hairstyle.

Why stop?

As if stopping were decorative.

But when your body depends on something just to feel neutral… When your nervous system panics without it… When you are risking seizures, blackouts, heart failure…

The question isn't why stop.

It's how are you still alive?

I didn't stop because I felt holy.

I stopped because I felt hunted.

I stopped when I realized I wasn't choosing the drink anymore — the drink was choosing me.

It waited for mania. It waited for grief. It waited for boredom. It waited for silence.

It knew my diagnosis by name.

That's not romance.

That's bondage.

And bondage doesn't always come with chains you can see.

Sometimes it comes in a stemmed glass.

What finally broke the cycle wasn't willpower.

It was accumulation.

My mother gone.

My father's heart failing.

The realization that I was becoming unreliable inside my own life.

The fear of losing custody — not legally, but spiritually.

Lose trust.

Lose dignity.

Lose myself.

Addiction is erosion.

Not explosion.

You don't notice the cliff disappearing beneath you until you're dangling.

And I was dangling.

I didn't break the chain because I felt strong.

I broke it because I was exhausted.

I was done dying in installments.

Recovery wasn't beautiful.

My hands shook. My sleep fractured. My moods spiked and crashed without anesthesia to buffer them.

But clarity?

Clarity returned in small pieces.

And I'd take small and real over big and false any day.

That was the day the bottle lost its power.

Not because alcohol became evil — but because I became aware.

And awareness is louder than craving.

Recovery didn't come wrapped in applause. It came in small disciplines. Medication. Therapy. Journals. Tracking triggers. Refusing isolation. Learning the difference between an episode and a craving.

I had to accept something uncomfortable: medication can stabilize you, but it cannot choose for you. Therapy can guide you, but it cannot surrender for you.

Coping skills stopped being suggestions and became survival code.

I stopped separating the diagnoses like rival cousins at a funeral.

Dually diagnosed.

Bipolar and addiction.

Living in the same body.

Fighting for control of the same nervous system.

And I had to name that war correctly before I could win anything.

Lipstick was the armor.

Addiction was the anesthesia.

And neither of them were peace.

Peace required direction.

Not perfection.

Direction.

Choosing breath over blackout.

Choosing pause over performance.

Choosing pen over pour.

That's the difference.

This wasn't about looking healed.

It was about being aligned.

And that alignment didn't come from glamour.

It came from honesty.

Right now, the bottle isn't my lover. I divorced it.

Not with guarantees — with intention.

There were years when alcohol occupied every thought.

Now I occupy my life.

I stay present.

I refuse to romanticize what once tried to consume me.

I didn't break the chains perfectly. I broke them deliberately.

Sobriety didn't give me perfection. It gave me my life back.

And that is not a small thing.

This is recovery in motion.

Sobriety without show.

Bipolar without apology.

Not perfection — direction.

I'm still walking it.

Still choosing it.

Healing doesn't come easy after the storm.

Soft isn't weakness.

Sometimes it's a slice of cheesecake.

Chapter 12: Prodigal Daughter

Anointed After the Fall

Everybody knows the story of the prodigal son.

The golden boy who walked away from everything.

Burned through inheritance.

Crawled back to mercy.

It's preached from pulpits, quoted in devotionals, dramatized like a cautionary tale about rebellion and redemption.

But nobody ever stops and asks—

What about the daughter?

What about the woman who walks out quietly?

Who doesn't storm off with inheritance, but drifts away in pieces.

Who doesn't demand her portion — but slowly trades it for survival.

I grew up in faith.

Not rigid. Not fire-and-brimstone. Not iron-skirted and trembling.

But steady.

Church wasn't performance in my house — it was rhythm. Sunday mornings. Weeknight Bible study. Music echoing through living rooms. My mother standing in conviction and compassion. Faith wasn't fear-based. It was grounding.

And still, faith doesn't make you immune to detours.

I didn't wake up one day and decide to "leave home."

I just kept walking.

Into ambition. Into diagnosis. Into trying to outwork bipolar and outthink depression. Into believing I could manage everything if I just stayed polished enough.

And yes — into that damn bottle when the noise got louder than my coping skills.

Not because I hated God. Not because I rejected faith.

Because I was exhausted.

Tired of being strong in public. Tired of being layered and labeled. Tired of carrying expectations that were never negotiated with my nervous system.

The prodigal daughter doesn't always rebel.

Sometimes she just survives too long without rest.

She smiles through the unraveling. She keeps credentials intact. She keeps lashes on. She keeps speaking well.

And internally? She is wandering.

The difference between the prodigal son and the prodigal daughter is this:

The son is framed as reckless.

The daughter is framed as disappointing.

There's a cultural silence around women who fall.

Especially Black women. Especially educated women. Especially women raised in faith.

We're supposed to manage. Sustain. Recover quietly. Return compliant.

But I didn't return quietly.

I returned informed.

Informed about my diagnosis.

Educated on my triggers.

Confronting cultural silence and inherited expectations.

Aware of what numbing costs.

Honest about what healing requires.

I did not come back to who I was.

I came back to who I survived becoming.

That's the difference.

My mother being a minister never meant I was protected from life. It meant I had language. It meant I had anchor. It meant I knew the difference between collapse and choice.

I went far.

Not geographically. Internally.

Far into over achievement. Far into exhaustion. Far into the idea that I could hold everything together if I just managed optics.

But here's what nobody tells you:

The fall is not always the worst part.

The pretending is.

The prodigal daughter doesn't return crawling.

She returns calibrated.

She returns sharper. Wiser. Aware of her nervous system. Aware of her thresholds. Aware of the cost of abandoning herself.

The anointing didn't happen before the fall.

It happened because of it.

Not church anointing. Not spotlight anointing.

Clarity.

Ownership.

Self-awareness.

I am not the minister's daughter trying to prove something.

I am a woman midlife. Mid-evolution. Mid-accountability. Mid-healing.

Still walking.

Still learning.

Still refusing to disappear.

I used to think coming back meant erasing what happened.

Like the miles didn't count.

Like the detours disqualified me.

Like the bruises meant I was damaged goods.

But detours aren't evidence of failure.

They're maps.

Every road I took — even the ones lit by impulse, exhaustion, ego, or pain — taught me something about my thresholds. My limits. My illusions. My strength.

I am not untouched by what I've been through.

I am marked by it.

And still, I am intact.

The prodigal son returned home.

The prodigal daughter returned to herself.

And that is the real resurrection.

Life tried to break me.

Instead it forged me.

-Scarred Gold

Chapter 13: Bruised, Not Broken

Not all bruises bloom on skin.

Some settle deep —

in the muscle of memory,

in the corners of your confidence,

in the quiet place where shame tries to nest.

You won't see them in photographs.

But I carried them in my posture.

In my hesitation.

In the way I avoided mirrors a little too long.

I wasn't shattered.

I was tender from impact.

And there's a difference.

People thought I was okay.

Because I could still articulate myself. Still show up when expected. Still wrap my truth in humor and lipstick.

But performance is not peace.

Behind the degrees, the mascara, the carefully chosen words
— I was recalibrating in private.

There's a specific kind of bruise that comes from surviving
yourself.

From manic ambition.

From depressive collapse.

From addiction long enough to realize it wasn't saving you —
only delaying the crash.

Bruised.

Not broken.

There's a dignity in that distinction.

Broken suggests irreparable. Bruised suggests healing in
progress.

And I had to choose which language I would use for myself.

After diagnosis. After denial.

After trying to out-intellect bipolar.

After trying to outrun anxiety.

After negotiating with that bottle like it was a business
partner instead of a thief.

I had to face something humbling:

Functioning is not the same as healed.

Sobriety is not the same as peace.

Smiling is not the same as wholeness.

Achievement is not the same as identity.

The bruises were internal.

Some days they looked like fatigue. Some days they looked like silence. Some days they looked like sitting still long enough to feel what I had been outrunning.

But bruises fade when oxygen reaches them.

And oxygen, for me, became truth.

Truth about my diagnosis. Truth about my triggers. Truth about what stigma had done to my self-image. Truth about being a Black woman labeled "too emotional" in a world already uncomfortable with our power.

I had to interrogate the word "broken."

Because society loves to break women. Especially Black women. Especially educated Black women. Especially women who were "supposed to know better."

But knowing better doesn't immunize you from biology. Or trauma. Or grief. Or chemical imbalance.

It just gives you language for the fight.

And I had that.

I studied what they called me. I researched what was mine. I separated trauma from temperament. I learned the rhythm of my mind instead of fearing it.

That's when bruised turned into informed.

That's when survival turned intentional.

Not glamorous. Not linear. Not Instagram-friendly.

Intentional.

Taking meds when I needed them. Going to therapy even when I hated unpacking. Canceling plans to protect my nervous system. Learning that peace doesn't mean I never shake — it means I know how to steady.

I stopped chasing "normal." I started chasing regulated.

There's freedom in that shift.

I don't need to be pristine. I don't need to be unscarred. I don't need to be what I was before diagnosis.

I just need to be intact.

And I am.

Still scarred. Still evolving. Still mid-journey.

But intact.

That's not broken.

That's battle-tested.

Healing taught me something else.

The path I thought I ruined wasn't ruined. It was rerouted.

And that rerouting wasn't punishment — it was instruction. Because sometimes the road you didn't plan is still the road. And sometimes the detour is the direction.

The road didn't fail me.

It just refused to be straight.

The curve wasn't punishment — it was

direction in disguise.

The detour rerouted my fear.

What I called a detour was the path

correcting itself.

Chapter 14: Detours Are Still Roads Too

The map burned.

The GPS failed.

The road cracked beneath my expectations.

And still — I walked.

What I thought was falling off course

was the beginning of my becoming.

Some roads don't look official. They aren't paved. They aren't applauded. They don't make sense on paper.

But they are roads.

And they count.

For a long time, I called my diagnosis a derailment.

A wrong turn. A catastrophic interruption. A deviation from the life I had planned so carefully.

I thought I had lost my path.

Law school dreams faded. Stability wavered. Relationships shifted. My own reflection felt unfamiliar.

That didn't look like progress.

It looked like a detour.

And detours, in our culture, feel like failure.

Especially for women taught to execute. Especially for Black women taught we can't afford mistakes.

But life doesn't operate in straight lines.

It loops. It bends. It stalls. It forces exits you didn't signal for.

And I learned something radical:

The detour is still movement.

Even when it feels like delay.

Even when it bruises your ego.

Even when it humbles you into silence.

The detour has terrain you were never going to see on the straight highway.

I met myself there.

Not the polished self. Not the performing self. Not the overachieving self.

The honest self.

The woman asking: what is the illness? What is me?

The woman deciding, I will not let a diagnosis define me more than my will.

The woman building a mental health toolbox because I understood something critical:

You don't survive long on reaction. You survive on preparation.

Triggers. Warning signs. Boundaries. Rituals. Breath. Silence. Movement. Rest.

These became road signs.

And slowly, I stopped saying:

"Why did this happen?"

I started saying:

"What is this teaching?"

That question changed the architecture of my life.

Because detours don't erase destination. They refine it.

I am not where I thought I would be.

But I am deeper than I ever was.

I am informed. I am calibrated. I am no longer chasing perfection. I am chasing alignment.

Hazard Lights

There were detours in my life that felt like pure hell.

Seasons where I didn't just lose direction — I lost the will to keep going. I didn't want to be here. Not metaphorically. Literally.

That's the part people don't like to talk about.

But something shifted.

Not all at once. Not dramatically. I just stopped trying to give up.

And I remember thinking:

If I'm going to be here, then damn it, I'm going to live.

Some days living looks heroic.

Some days living looks like brushing your teeth.

It's not glamorous. It's ADLs — activities of daily living.

Get out of bed.

Shower.

Coffee.

Move your body.

Open the blinds.

Depression isn't always loud. Sometimes it's a room that gets smaller and smaller until the bed feels like a prison.

Feeling your feelings is one thing.

But when the bed becomes your world for days at a time…

When isolation starts feeling like safety…

When dropping out of your own life becomes your coping mechanism —

That's not rest.

That's a warning.

And I had to learn the difference.

This is not an easy road with these diagnoses. There are mornings I wake up and the weight is still there. But I know now that staying still is not the solution.

Detours nearly took me out.

But they didn't end me.

They taught me that survival begins with the smallest rebellion:

Get. Up.

It took me twenty-five years to learn that lesson.

Staying in that space is not coping.

It's not just a season.

It's not personality.

It's erosion.

There is a difference between feeling your feelings and building a home inside them. I was building furniture in hell and calling it normal.

That's when I understood something.

If hell is a mindset, then the key is internal too.

So I snatched it back.

Hell had become my mind space.

And I decided I was done living there.

This is not a feel-good memoir.

This is my lived experience.

It hasn't been a roller coaster.

It hasn't been some poetic derailment.

The terrain has been hostile — unstable

ground demanding preparation.

And preparation means this:

If suicidal thoughts start circling, if ideation shows up, if I feel myself wanting to disappear or drop out of life, I do not negotiate with that space anymore.

I get a lifeline.

That is not weakness.

That is strategy.

That is survival matured into discipline.

That is what matters.

When someone drops out of life, when depression pulls them under, it is not always self-loathing. It is not laziness. It is not a failure of willpower. And it is not something you can just "get together."

For some of us — especially when navigating bipolar disorder — emotions are not light weather. They are full atmospheric systems.

What someone else might process as a passing bad day can become, for you, a full internal siege.

It is excess.

Weight that sits in your chest.

Noise beyond tolerance.

Intensity that doesn't ask permission.

Regulating your thoughts takes focus.

Separating truth from distortion takes clarity.

Holding the present moment takes everything — so you don't get swallowed whole.

It isn't drama.

It's volume.

And when that volume stays high long

enough,

it begins to consume —

first your energy,

then your mind space,

then your sense of proportion.

That is the hell I'm talking about.

Not self-hatred.

Neurological overwhelm.

An emotional system running at a frequency that does not power down on command.

That's different.

And pretending it isn't different is part of the stigma.

Awareness became non-negotiable.

And the tools in my toolbox became the architecture of my survival.

I'm no longer afraid to walk the road my life handed me.

But I'm no longer willing to walk it blindly either.

I demand new roads now —

roads built for the woman who understands.

Understanding changes everything.

Becoming isn't just growth. Becoming is knowing.

Knowing your triggers.

Owning your weaknesses.

Standing in your strength.

Recognizing when to pivot.

Refusing to keep negotiating with chaos.

And knowing — like we used to say — is only half the battle.

The other half is action.

It's refusing to ride the same merry-go-round just because it's familiar.

It's choosing new terrain.

Detours are still roads.

But you don't have to circle the same block forever.

I'm not afraid anymore.

I'm aware.

And awareness demands movement.

And that is a better road.

Sometimes we think redemption looks like returning to the original plan.

It doesn't.

Sometimes redemption looks like standing in the reroute and saying,

"This counts too."

The diagnosis counts. The addiction counts. The survival counts. The rebuilding counts.

All of it is road.

None of it is wasted.

Detours teach you where your foundation cracked.

Excavation teaches you how to rebuild it.

Because after you accept the reroute, after you realize the bruises didn't end you, after you understand the road still holds,

you have a choice.

You can keep walking surface-level.

Or you can dig.

And when I decided to dig, I wasn't looking for answers.

I was looking for fire.

Soul work ain't pretty.

It's flour on your hands, fire in the oven,

and patience long enough to let it brown just right.

Peace tastes like sweet potato pie — earned, not handed.

Chapter 15: Excavating the Fire

I thought the diagnosis was the fire —

the detonation,

the fault line ripping open beneath me.

But the real devastation wasn't the explosion.

It was the aftermath.

The repeated collapses.

The same crisis resurfacing under new disguises.

Heat that never fully cooled.

Ash that settled, then stirred again.

It wasn't dramatic enough to register as catastrophe.

But it was consistent — and that reshaped me.

Eventually, repetition stops feeling accidental.

It stops feeling like a "season."

It starts demanding attention.

At some point, you either keep calling it a phase —

or you admit something is burning underneath it all.

That's when excavation began.

There was no blueprint for how to live with being dually diagnosed.

No example standing in front of me saying, *I carried this ache - and my life didn't stop.*

No one modeling what diagnosis looked like without shrinking — and still rising.

No one showing me you could unravel, rebuild, and become powerful anyway.

I didn't have a template.

I had to become the example.

I don't talk about therapy the way I used to.

Not because I don't believe in it.

Not because I didn't sit in those rooms and tell the truth.

Not because it didn't help. It did.

Therapy didn't teach me how to reinvent myself.

It taught me how to reclaim the woman I was before the noise, the labels, the coping, and the survival mode that swallowed my voice.

Therapy mattered.

But what saved me was what happened beyond it — before and after the session ended.

I still had to live inside my own mind.

And take responsibility for what lived there.

That is soul work.

And I do not use that phrase lightly.

Soul work is not a rejection of therapy.

It is not a dismissal of medication, psychology, or science.

It is the translation of all of it into something I could actually live with.

Something that honored my ancestry,

my culture,

my spirituality.

My lived reality as a Black woman navigating mental illness in a world that does not make room for our softness.

In communities like mine, mental health was not framed as care.

It was framed as weakness.

You pray.

You push.

You perform.

You survive.

No slowing down long enough to unpack your own mind.

No interrogating your wounds.

Definitely no admitting you're unraveling — because unraveling sounds too much like failure.

And failure was never presented as an option.

But here is the truth we were never handed:

What you refuse to face does not disappear.

It waits — in your patterns, your triggers, in the emergency you swear came out of nowhere.

That's when I understood the fire wasn't the ending – it was the doorway.

Soul work is the quiet, unglamorous labor of learning how to live with yourself.

It is choosing awareness over avoidance.

Presence over escape.

Truth over numbing. Care over chaos.

It does not happen on stages.

It does not happen for applause.

It does not announce itself with dramatic music.

It happens at 3 a.m. when your thoughts turn against you and you decide to breathe anyway.

It happens when your hands are shaking and you reach for a pen instead of a bottle.

It happens when you name a trigger before it names you.

When you interrupt a spiral before it owns you.

When you cancel the performance and choose alignment instead.

Seeing It Is the First Act of Survival

There was a point where I realized the real work did not begin in a therapist's office. It began earlier — quietly inside my own mind. The first doorway wasn't a door at all. It was honesty. Before help. Before language caught up. Before diagnosis became something I could explain.

It began with permission.

Permission to think the thought.

Permission to sit with it without panic.

Permission to have an honest conversation with myself without immediately trying to fix, label, or silence it.

Most people are never taught that part. We move quickly toward solutions because discomfort feels dangerous. But before awareness comes change. If we don't let thoughts surface, we never learn which ones need care — and which ones need to pass.

Listening to yourself is not weakness. It is discernment. A discipline of staying present long enough to understand what your mind is signaling.

Acknowledging pain is not surrender. It is information. And that recognition changed everything.

I know more now — not because someone handed me a manual, but because I survived the absence of one.

Silence does not protect you.

Being unseen does not save you.

It isolates you long enough for suffering to grow roots.

You have to face it —

even when it threatens your pride,

even when it disrupts the story you were raised to protect.

You can't heal what you refuse to acknowledge.

You can't solve what you pretend is not happening.

Ignoring the storm did not make me strong.

It made the storm louder.

Naming it changed everything. The moment I stopped denying what was happening inside me was the moment survival became strategy.

That wasn't weakness.

That was reclamation.

You don't find your way out of the dark by pretending it isn't there.

You find it by standing still long enough to say:

This mind.

This life.

This spirit.

Is worth fighting for.

Twenty-five years is a long time to circle the same fire.

At some point, survival stops being noble. It becomes repetitive — a loop, a carousel playing the same song while you age in the middle of it.

And I don't want that life anymore.

I want more.

Not just thriving.

Not just managing.

Not just stabilizing.

More.

You have to want something different than the chaos.
Hunger for a self not built on surviving disaster.

For years, I fed the label.

Studied it.

Argued with it.

Wore it.

Fought it.

But you can only orbit a diagnosis for so long before you ask:

Is this living?

There may not be a yellow brick road. No wizard. No
shortcut.

But there is a road back —

back to yourself,

back to dignity,

back to becoming.

Detours are still roads.

Life isn't linear. It isn't straight.

But you do get a say in how you steer it.

"Live.

Strive.

Thrive."

That was never a slogan.

It was a standard.

It is a standard.

Because after twenty-five years, I don't just want to survive the storm.

I want a life that feels intentional.

This chapter of my life is not about applause. It's about ownership. I studied my own life like it was a case file. I tracked my patterns. I examined what hurt me, what stabilized me, what nearly destroyed me.

Not the kind of ownership that draws attention — the kind that steadies you when no one is watching. The kind that teaches you when to pause, when to move, when to move forward without asking permission. Alignment became my anchor, not to impress the world, but to return to myself and keep going.

Therapy gave me language. Ownership made me accountable for how I used it. Understanding is one thing. Living it — consistently, quietly — is another.

Therapy gave me language.

Recovery gave me structure.

Soul work gave me ownership.

Healing is my practice.

Stability is something I maintain.

Sanity is soul work.

It is the ongoing responsibility of tending to your inner life so you do not collapse under the weight of living.

Everything else — peace, balance, clarity — grows out of that discipline.

For me, soul work became daily inventory.

Every morning, I stand in front of the mirror — not performing for anyone — and say, "Hello, gorgeous. Let's begin."

Not out of ego.

Out of grounding.

I remind myself to be gentle — because I am carrying more than most people will ever see.

I speak my motto aloud: live. strive. thrive.

That is not branding.

It is strategy.

I reinforce positive self-talk because my mind has known chaos.

I readjust my thought patterns because I have lived the consequences of not doing so.

People think healing is loud.

It is not.

Healing is intentional.

Healing is choosing yourself again after the fire.

Not perfection.

Not applause.

Just staying.

Breath by breath.

I am still here.

That is the win.

Soul work is how a Black woman survives inside systems not built for her.

It is what remains beyond diagnosis — where ancestry, education, intuition, accountability, faith and grit carry the work forward.

It is how I learned I am not my diagnosis —

and I do not have to deny it to reclaim my power.

I did not accept labels blindly.

I interrogated them.

I researched them.

I asked: What is the illness? What is trauma? What is me?

That sorting took years.

Decades.

It required brutal honesty and discipline.

But somewhere in that excavation, I stopped looking for answers.

And started looking for fire.

The fire that was already there.

Not the chaos fire.

The refining fire.

The fire that clarifies instead of consumes.

You can keep walking circles around your pain.

Or you can dig.

Not to destroy yourself.

But to recover what was buried.

This is that work.

Not glamorous.

Not performative.

Not casual.

Serious.

Lived.

Maintained.

Soul work is how I stopped running from my own mind.

It is how I learned that therapy is one tool on the survival menu — not the entire meal.

It is how I moved from crisis to consciousness.

And consciousness saved my life.

Because this was never about becoming someone else.

It was about remembering who the hell I was.

And choosing — everyday — to live fully awake.

There's a difference between celebration and anesthesia.

I learned it the hard way.

I wasn't glamorous.

Some nights, I was surviving.

Survival came in a glass.

Not pleasure.

Not luxury.

Just getting to morning.

Survival isn't pretty.

It's measured by what you reach for

when the room gets quiet.

I didn't call it coping.

I called it making it to morning.

Survival has a taste.

I knew it by heart.

Chapter 16: Sipping on Survival

Some sip to celebrate.

I sipped to survive.

The bottle blurred more than my vision. It blurred my life. What looked like coping was erosion dressed in lipstick and denial.

Putting the bottle down was one of the most decisive moves I've ever made. Not for applause. Not for performance. For clarity. For custody of my own mind.

It put me back in the driver's seat.

Motherhood sharpened. Decisions steadied. My thinking stopped slurring into tomorrow. For the first time in a long time, I could feel myself returning — piece by sober piece.

I was tired of not showing up.

Tired of checking out while pretending to check in.

Tired of drunken detachment disguised as stress relief.

Tired of telling myself "It's not that bad," while everything quietly deteriorated.

I had to get tired enough to stop.

That wasn't cliché — it was survival math. Either I stopped, or I lost everything.

There were nights I felt like a captive in my own body. Not dramatic. Not performative. Captive. The bottle dictated my movements, my moods, my mornings. It decided who I called, what I ruined, how I showed up.

In my mind, I envisioned myself chained to it — dragged across the dark waters of my own making.

Metaphorically, it felt like the Middle Passage. Not poetic exaggeration.

When I reference the Middle Passage, I do so with full awareness of its magnitude. I use it to convey the dominance the bottle had in my life — that's how enslaved I felt.

I felt as if my mind boarded a ship I never meant to step onto. Suddenly I was cargo — stripped of autonomy, dignity, direction.

That's not for shock value.

That's how it felt.

It was a beast with an insatiable appetite.

The bottle was not leisure.

It was a mutiny.

It rewrote my days.

It redrew my character.

It stole my sovereignty.

DUI. Broken trust. Jobs compromised. Relationships fractured. My son watching a version of me I never intended to become.

That's not dramatic language.

That's inventory.

If you don't remember your last rock bottom, you haven't hit it yet.

Because when you truly hit bottom, it engraves you. It brands you into consciousness. You don't forget it. It wakes you up or it buries you.

I chose wake-up.

Putting the bottle down was not a motivational speech moment. It was practical warfare. I built rituals. I tracked triggers. I replaced chaos with structure.

Some mornings survival looked like this:

– My medication poured in a dish instead of wine in a glass.

– Pen to paper. One honest sentence before the world touched me.

– A pause before reaction.

– A check-in with reality.

And no, it wasn't glamorous.

But it was sovereignty.

Addiction had been a tyrant. Sobriety was not ease — it was command. I became the captain of my own ship again. I reclaimed my coordinates. I stopped negotiating with something that had proven itself untrustworthy.

The bottle had written too many chapters of my life.

I took the pen back.

Now when people ask what I'm sipping on?

Clarity.

Accountability.

Presence.

Survival — with a twist of grace.

And this is where the work deepens.

Because survival is not the same as living.

And I was finally ready to tell that truth.

Coping can dress like comfort.

It can pour like relief.

It slips in at midnight and tells you this is enough.

Just make it through tonight.

And sometimes that whisper feels like love.

Survival begins as necessity.

I didn't call it hiding.

It became my lover.

It kept me alive —

but it also taught me how to shrink.

Chapter 17: Seduced by Survival

I made survival look seductive.

Head high.

Answers ready.

Strong in public.

Cracking jokes.

Handling business.

They called it resilience.

But survival is deceptive when you mistake endurance for elevation.

I wasn't living.

I was existing.

Floating through days.

Grinding through nights.

Running on adrenaline and denial.

Survival had become my default setting.

It kept me breathing — but it didn't teach me how to thrive.

That's the seduction.

You convince yourself that "not dead" equals success.

You measure progress by catastrophe avoided instead of joy lived.

You tell yourself, "At least I'm functioning."

Functioning is not flourishing.

Survival mode made chaos familiar. Crisis felt normal. Stability felt foreign. Live long enough in volatility and peace feels suspicious.

That's what nobody prepares you for.

I didn't just battle addiction.

I battled identity erosion.

I battled sleepless nights where insomnia sat beside me like a co-conspirator.

I battled manic surges and depressive collapses that made reality feel negotiable.

Sleep abandoned me.

Thoughts multiplied.

Nights stretched like interrogation rooms.

And when survival becomes your only language, you don't reach for healing — you reach for what keeps you conscious.

I believed I was strong because I endured.

But endurance alone is not power.

Here's the hinge:

Soul work stabilized me.

Sobriety cleared me.

But surviving wasn't enough.

I had to decide to live differently.

There was a day I looked in the mirror and didn't recognize the woman staring back. Not because she was broken — but because she was muted.

Muted ambition.

Muted softness.

Muted joy.

I remembered the girl who majored in international business. The woman who moved with fire in her walk. The mind that could focus, build, create.

Survival had reduced me to maintenance.

And I wanted more than maintenance.

That's when the question shifted:

Not "How do I survive this?"

But

"Who do I become beyond it?"

Survival kept me alive.

But it never taught me how to expand.

Healing began when I stopped glamorizing endurance and started demanding alignment.

Not applause.

Not redemption arcs.

Not sainthood.

Alignment.

With my values.

With my responsibilities.

With my son.

With my mind.

Survival seduced me into thinking barely breathing was enough.

I am not here to barely breathe.

I am here to build.

And once you realize that survival is only step one, you can no longer hide inside it.

That's when evolution became necessary.

Healing isn't magic.

It's maintenance.

The woman I fought to become didn't appear overnight.

She was assembled.

I stopped waiting to be rescued.

I built a toolbox instead.

Chapter 18: Tools Don't Apologize

This is lived healing — not packaged positivity.

Handcrafted tools, built when survival alone wasn't enough.

Nobody hands you peace.

Nobody teaches you how to quiet a mind that will not rest

or how to breathe when your chest feels like it's collapsing.

You learn because you have to.

You learn because the alternative costs too much.

Rituals became structure.

Not superstition — stabilization.

Not performance — grounding.

Soul work was the quiet labor of learning my own mind.

It translated clinical language into lived reality.

It taught me how to carry what I survived without letting it carry me.

Therapy named it.

Recovery steadied it.

Soul work made it sustainable.

These are the tools that kept me here.

Not trendy wellness talk.

Not aesthetic rituals.

Real-world tools you reach for when you're breaking.

Some days it was breathwork.

Some days it was music loud enough to interrupt the spiral.

Some days it was rest — especially when I felt I didn't deserve it.

And some nights, it was choosing not to self-destruct when nobody was watching.

That's when strength stopped meaning silence.

That's when practice became protection.

The toolbox became my response to collapse — structure, awareness, interruption, a deliberate pause.

Survival wasn't accidental.

It was practiced.

Coping is not weakness.

Coping is how you stay alive long enough to heal.

Not Every Lifeline Is Loud

Not every lifeline comes with sirens.

Sometimes it's a quiet walk at dawn.

A journal waiting by the bed.

A playlist that steadies your breathing.

Music wasn't entertainment.

It was medicine when words failed.

This isn't about perfection.

It's about preservation.

Survival isn't a one-time act.

It's a daily discipline.

When I committed to these tools — therapy, medication, prayer, structure — I began to see possibility again.

I didn't just exist.

I engaged.

I stabilized.

I expanded.

The Hard Truth

When I was intoxicated — clouded by alcohol and despair — I couldn't see clearly.

Not my son.

Not myself.

The distortion wasn't outside me.

It was internal.

Hopelessness blurred my vision.

The bottle grew louder than my own voice.

Breaking that cycle required tools — emotional, physical, spiritual.

The most powerful one was self-awareness.

Knowing my triggers.

Tracking my moods.

Recognizing when bipolar was pulling me too high or too low.

Preparing before the storm made landfall became essential.

These tools aren't theories.

They are lifelines.

Anchors.

Infrastructure.

My Mental Health Toolbox

Journaling

Music therapy

Sunlight and nature walks

Gratitude practice

Safe social connections

Hotline numbers saved and accessible

Prayer, meditation, reflection

Daily mental check-ins

Am I okay today?

If not, what do I need?

Who can I call?

How do I reset?

When I couldn't answer, that was my signal to reach out —
not retreat.

The Hardest Tool: Rest

Rest challenged me the most.

Not because I didn't need it.

Because I didn't trust it.

When survival has been your default setting, stillness feels
undeserved.

But the body keeps its records.

Eventually, it demands recalibration.

Rest wasn't quitting.

It was regulation.

Sometimes the bravest thing I did was not pushing through.

It was lying down and allowing recovery.

This isn't decorative self-care.

This is nervous-system repair.

This is preservation.

My toolbox didn't come from a store.

It came from trauma, relapse, therapy, reckoning.

Every tool was earned.

Every tool was survival turned deliberate.

You don't have to be perfect to move forward.

You don't have to be finished to be functional.

You have to begin.

Every day I show up for myself is intentional.

Every tool I use is agency over despair.

Healing doesn't have a finish line.

It has rhythm.

Soul work isn't candles and mood lighting.

It's consistency.

It's self-honesty.

It's asking the hard questions before things spiral.

Breathwork slowed my thoughts.

Structure slowed my reactions.

Awareness slowed my collapse.

Healing doesn't happen in chaos.

It happens in safety.

Safety doesn't always look like a straight road.

The one I trusted most was already beginning to crack.

There was no yellow brick road.

Redemption looked like dirt under my nails

and blisters on my feet.

No wizard.

No rescue.

Just the space between the version I performed

and the woman I am.

Chapter 19: Yellow Brick Road to Redemption

I followed the Yellow Brick Road like it promised me safety.

Education. Achievement. Applause.

I thought arrival meant healing.

I thought success meant stability.

But Emerald Cities are built on illusion,

and wizards hide behind curtains.

The road glittered.

My spirit did not.

And when the shine wore off,

I wasn't angry —

I was grieving.

Not just my losses.

My illusions.

For a long time, I thought my life was the Yellow Brick Road.

Shining.

Promising.

Linear.

Step here. Achieve this. Win that.

But real life doesn't hand you ruby slippers.

It hands you diagnoses.

Expectations.

Loss.

And sometimes, the only thing more disorienting than the storm is realizing you can't go back to the version of yourself

who stepped into it.

Everyone loves a clear path.

A glittering trail.

A future flawless on paper.

People love to build Yellow Brick Roads for you.

They lay expectations like stones — shiny, impressive, strategic.

Walk here.

Graduate there.

Lead this.

Become that.

And if you stay on the path — everyone applauds.

But what nobody prepares you for is what happens when your mind doesn't cooperate with the road map.

There were expectations for my life long before I understood their weight — not small ones. Big. Brilliant. The kind spoken over you before you've even decided who you are.

Not cruel expectations. Loving. Protective. Prophetic.

My mother saw something in me before the world did.

She named it. She nurtured it. She defended it.

And every time my illness tried to interrupt the narrative —

every time the pendulum swung too far

or the cracks in my armor became visible —

she found another road.

When one path collapsed, she helped me build a new one.

Another program.

Another degree.

Another certification.

Another reinvention.

She refused to let me believe that a diagnosis was a dead end.

She refused to let me sit inside the wreckage.

But here's what nobody talks about —

Reinvention can look like resilience.

But it can also hide exhaustion.

Sometimes reinvention isn't evolution.

Sometimes it's survival dressed up in ambition.

Every time I rebuilt, tiny fractures formed in my armor.

Not visible to the world.

Just to me.

Living with diagnoses isn't just clinical.

It's existential.

It makes you question your worth.

Your stamina.

Your destiny.

It makes you wonder:

Am I chasing my purpose —

or trying to prove I still belong in the room?

The world sees potential.

You feel pressure.

The world sees promise.

You feel fracture.

And when the wheels keep wobbling beneath you —

you start asking yourself dangerous questions:

Am I becoming who I'm meant to be…

or just performing who they expect me to be?

That's where the real unraveling begins.

The road to reinvention can become exhausting.

When the expectations are high and your mind won't cooperate,

you begin to question not your effort —

but your worth.

Are you weak?

Are you behind?

Are you broken?

Or are you just trying to survive something invisible?

I wasn't wandering aimlessly.

I was wandering strategically.

Trying to find the version of myself that could carry both ambition and illness.

Both faith and fracture.

Both brilliance and burnout.

The world called it potential.

Inside, nothing felt steady.

I tried to be the image people believed in.

Tried to outrun the diagnosis.

Tried to perform stability.

And somewhere inside that performance,

I started losing the mirror.

Because my mother was the mirror.

She saw me clearly — even when I couldn't see myself.

When she looked at me, I wasn't bipolar.

I wasn't a setback.

I wasn't a disappointment.

I was her daughter.

And when you lose the only person who reflected your truest self back to you —

you don't just lose a parent.

You lose your anchor.

Your coordinates.

The road signs that quietly told you:

You're still you.

I thought losing a version of myself at twenty-two was the hardest loss I'd endure. I hadn't yet learned what it meant to lose the woman who held my reflection steady. She was always there to re-route the map — to show me how to return to myself.

I didn't realize what it would mean to navigate without her.

The Yellow Brick Road wasn't glittering anymore. It was cracked pavement.

And for the first time, I wasn't reinventing myself.

I was trying not to disappear.

Grief was coming.

Not as an emotion.

As a landscape.

And I had never walked that terrain before.

Grief isn't a moment.

It's a battlefield.

Some days I lose ground; some days I win inches.

Losing my mother didn't just break my heart — it rewired it.

You don't get over grief.

You negotiate with it.

You live beside it.

Some days you forgive yourself for still hurting.

I don't dust it off.

I carry it like a scar that still remembers.

That's not broken — that's bonded.

Chapter 20: Grief Is Terrain

Dear Grief…

In an imperfect world, how do I reclaim joy when the woman who gave me life also held my spirit steady —

is no longer here to anchor my storm?

My mother was more than my compass —

she was my church, my truth, my soft place to land.

She loved with a God-light so pure it could see beauty even in brokenness. She was the current beneath my stillness.

She was the quiet rhythm beneath my chaos. The steady heartbeat under my ambition.

And now… I'm here.

Trying to walk, breathe, live with half my soul missing.

So I ask you, Grief —

what now?

What do I do with all this fire in my belly, this story in my bones, this dream she and I birthed together —

Whiskey Prayers?

Because I don't just want to survive this. I want to turn pain into something sacred —

without needing a pulpit.

Grief is bittersweet.

That's not a metaphor. It's a taste.

It lingers.

It coats everything.

It never fully leaves the taste buds.

It shows up in the back of the throat when you laugh too hard.

In the pause before a celebration.

In the quiet when the house goes still.

The pain doesn't go away.

The hole doesn't close.

You just learn how to breathe around it.

That ache isn't dramatic.

It's steady.

Subtle.

Like weather that never quite clears.

Grief doesn't ask permission. It interrupts.

It bends time, distorts memory, and reshapes the way you exist in your own body. You don't come out of it untouched. You come out altered.

Altered in posture.

Altered in tolerance.

Altered in what matters.

For a long time, I thought strength meant silence.

I thought surviving meant not letting it show — swallowing the pain, dressing it up, keeping it moving.

But silence isn't safety.

It's pressure building.

And pressure doesn't disappear just because no one can see it.

It compounds.

It calcifies.

It waits for fracture.

Somewhere between the break and the rebuilding, I started to recognize patterns — what was grief, what was illness, what was learned survival. I began to understand that not everything needed fixing, but everything needed naming.

Naming is power.

When you name a thing, it stops haunting you in the dark.

Insight doesn't come all at once.

You sip it. Slowly. Carefully.

You learn what parts of you hardened to survive.

You learn what parts went quiet to stay alive.

You learn what you carried because no one taught you how to put it down.

Life keeps coming — bills, relationships, expectations — even when you're still bleeding internally. And the world doesn't pause while you figure out how to breathe again.

So you learn to live anyway.

Not healed.

Not finished.

Just aware.

Awareness is not weakness.

It's recalibration.

This is where surviving shifts from reaction to recognition.

This is where the breaking becomes the beginning of insight.

Grief is hard terrain. You can't prepare for it.

No one prepares you for the aftermath.

Not the loss —

the living after the loss.

The birthdays without her voice.

The decisions without her counsel.

The victories without her nod of approval.

Grief doesn't end. It restructures your life.

The work isn't moving on.

The work is learning how to live forward while grief stays present — not in the foreground, but in the background of your mind.

That distinction matters.

Grief isn't an emotion you resolve.

It's terrain you learn how to navigate.

Some days require momentum.

Some days require restraint.

Both are movement.

What people call "healing" often looks like disappearance.

Silence. Withdrawal. Containment.

But stillness isn't always safety.

Sometimes it's fear sitting still long enough to look responsible.

Grief taught me something no diagnosis ever did:

timing is survival.

Knowing when to move.

Knowing when to pause.

Knowing when forcing progress costs more than it gives.

Loss doesn't fade — it integrates.

It informs how you walk, what you carry, what you no longer rush. It changes your pace. The ache doesn't disappear. It becomes part of the landscape. And once you stop fighting the terrain, you stop wasting energy trying to be who you were before.

Because you can't go back.

You can only integrate forward.

Grief is not a setback.

It's a recalibration.

I don't move around grief anymore.

I move with it.

It walks beside me.

It informs me.

But it does not own me.

That's how I stay upright.

That's how I keep going.

Grief is terrain.

And I have learned how to walk it.

I've always believed mental health awareness should be universally sexy

——

not glossy, not trivial, but accessible.

We have to change the way we educate, perceive, and digest mental illness.

When language becomes human, stigma weakens.

Chapter 21: Learning to Carry the Ache

The language of therapy missed me long before I ever rejected it.

Twenty-five years ago, therapy didn't sound like something built for people like me. Not because I was unwilling to heal, but because the language didn't reflect how my community survives.

It omitted the cultural muscles we've relied on for generations: resilience, faith, grit, adaptation, pride.

When language fails to recognize how a people have learned to endure, it loses them before it ever reaches them.

The minute the words feel foreign, the mind closes. If identity isn't welcome at the table, healing feels like exile. And exile looks like resistance to people who never had to hide.

Healing can't begin if the door never opens.

That omission turned me away. I told myself Black folks don't do this — not because we don't feel pain, but because pain has never been a luxury for us.

We survived by moving forward.

Not by sitting still with feelings we were never taught how to hold safely.

What I see now is different. Not perfect — but different.

Conversations are opening. More of us are naming what we once carried silently.

And when therapy respects culture instead of erasing it, it becomes less of a threat and more of a tool.

It isn't about race as a barrier.

It's about recognition.

Mental health shouldn't feel like interrogation.

It should feel like permission.

Healing works best when it speaks in a voice the soul already understands.

When that voice feels foreign, the mind closes before healing begins.

When it didn't recognize my story, I didn't recognize it as safety.

I was surrounded — yet internally isolated.

Once I stopped trying to speak their language, I started listening to my own, and everything I'd been holding split wide open.

The ache wasn't alone because I withdrew.

It was alone because survival required silence.

This understanding didn't come overnight.

It came from more than twenty-five years of therapy — trial and error, learning and unlearning, surviving and evolving.

It came from navigating a system that was never designed with women who look like me in mind. When I was first diagnosed, there were few resources, fewer conversations, and almost no culturally relevant framework to help me make sense of what I was facing.

So I stayed. I listened. I learned. I questioned. I pushed back when something didn't sit right. I took what worked. I discarded what didn't. Slowly, deliberately, I built a life that made sense to me.

And building it required awareness – not perfection.

Staying aware of my stress and knowing when to reach out wasn't weakness.

It was intention.

It was survival.

Done on purpose.

It was a shift from reacting to my life to responding to it.

There was no blueprint.

No template.

No one modeling how to survive this without shrinking.

So I became the example.

That's why I share this now - not as theory, not as a professional credential, but as lived experience.

The greatest lesson I've learned wasn't how to fix my feelings. It was how to feel them without letting them run my life. It wasn't about control. It was about capacity – learning to feel and keep moving.

Therapy has been useful in my life. At times, it saved me. At other times, it stretched me past my comfort. And over time, it taught me how to return to myself.

This perspective only comes with time — and I offer it with honesty, not perfection.

For many Black people and people of color, mental health isn't just a diagnosis.

It's a cultural confrontation.

Not because we don't believe in healing.

Not because we don't love our people.

But because we were raised on survival.

We were taught to endure.

To push through.

To pray.

To handle our business.

Strength wasn't optional. It was inherited.

Silence wasn't avoidance. It was protection.

When Diagnosis Feels Like a Verdict

When I was diagnosed more than twenty-five years ago, my family wasn't prepared — not because they didn't care, but because none of us had been taught how to hold this.

We had no language for bipolar disorder beyond stigma.

I understood counseling academically.

I knew the difference between psychology and psychiatry.

But when the diagnosis became mine?

It didn't feel clinical.

It felt terminal.

Like someone had spoken a death sentence over my identity.

Not support — a sentence.

Not information — a scarlet letter.

In communities built on overcoming, admitting pain can feel dangerous.

Strength becomes currency.

Resilience becomes identity.

And anything that threatens that identity feels like erosion.

Cultural Silence Is Not Ignorance

What I've learned since is this:

Our resistance wasn't about ignorance.

It was about strategy.

We descend from people who survived slavery, segregation, displacement, systemic neglect. Our nervous systems carry history. Survival instincts are ancestral.

Silence was currency.

It kept us safe.

But what once protected us can become heavy when there is no place to soften.

Mental health conversations often felt foreign — clinical language with no cultural translation. Help that didn't account for context. Frameworks that didn't see the whole story.

And if you don't see yourself reflected in the room, it's hard to rest in it.

It Isn't Just Culture. It's Access

It isn't just stigma.

It's layered.

Education determines exposure.

Those with proximity to academic or professional language around mental health understand therapy differently than those without it. Not because they're smarter — but because they've been introduced to it.

And then there's insurance.

You can believe in getting help and still not afford it.

You can want support and still face waitlists, denials, or minimal care.

Quality changes with coverage.

Representation changes with geography.

Access isn't equal.

So resistance isn't always denial.

Sometimes it's survival.

Choosing between rent and therapy.

Childcare and medication.

Shame and vulnerability.

These layers — culture, class, education, access — stack on top of each other.

If we don't name them, we end up blaming people for systems that were never built to catch them.

Strength Without Support Becomes Isolation

For a long time, mental health wasn't just uncomfortable in my community — it was a liability.

You didn't talk about it openly.

You whispered.

You prayed.

You endured.

Strength was the badge.

But strength without support becomes isolation.

Silence doesn't erase pain.

It stores it.

It piles up.

It leaks sideways.

And eventually — it demands payment.

We are losing people not because help doesn't exist, but because shame convinces them they should survive without it.

Help feels like surrender in a culture that prides itself on overcoming.

But here's what I had to learn the hard way:

Seeking support isn't surrender.

It's strategy.

Therapy is not betrayal.

Medication is not erasure.

Prayer and psychiatry are not enemies.

They are tools.

And strength is sustained by tools.

Survival Had to Evolve

For years, my medication was wrong.

My voice was buried under shame.

But I kept learning.

Detour by detour.

Because healing isn't one road.

And detours are roads too.

Finding what worked required participation.

Not blind trust.

Not silence.

Participation.

I had to track patterns.

Learn my chemistry.

Speak up when something wasn't right.

Advocate for myself.

Healing required involvement.

Eventually, I became conscious of things I would never have recognized without these experiences.

That is not a consolation prize.

That is evolution.

What the Ache Actually Is

The ache is not one emotion.

It is cumulative.

Grief layered with expectation.

Strength layered with shame.

Survival layered with silence.

The ache was carried alone, even when people were around.

The ache wasn't invisible.

It just wasn't culturally welcomed.

I didn't suffer in silence because I wanted to.

Silence was what survival required.

And survival kept me alive — but it never taught me how to live.

There is a difference.

The Shift

This isn't an argument against resilience.

It's an invitation.

An invitation to stop carrying the ache alone.

Not by abandoning who we are —

but by expanding the ways we care for ourselves.

Faith taught us how to survive oppression.

Therapy can teach us how to lay down burdens.

That's not weakness.

That's evolution.

The conversation is changing.

Slowly.

Dinner table by dinner table.

And strength does not have to be silent to be real.

The ache is not something I aim to erase.

It's something I've learned to carry with wisdom.

With boundaries.

With agency.

Not submission.

I am not defined by what hurt me.

I am defined by the fact that I learned how to carry it — without letting it name me.

I used to call them midnight sessions

—

the hour when the world slept and my demons stayed wide awake.

Bourbon on the table. Music low.

I called it my come-to-Jesus time — whiskey prayers whispered into the dark,

drowning sorrow while calling its reflection.

It felt spiritual.

It felt honest.

But it was still survival dressed up as a ritual.

Now my midnight looks different.

The music stays.

The honesty stays.

The bottle does not.

I find my center without pouring myself under.

I sit with the thoughts instead of silencing them.

Midnight is still sacred —

but now it's where I heal, not where I hide.

✦ ✦ ✦

Chapter 22: Midnight Draws Near, Still I Rise

I don't fear midnight anymore.

I respect it.

Midnight is where the unspoken waits.

Where the noise thins out and the truth steps forward.

Where there is no applause. No audience.

Just me — and what's left of the day.

Midnight is sacred and dangerous at the same time.

It's the hour where anxiety runs laps.

Midnight stopped being a playground for sabotage.

It became a checkpoint.

Where regret replays conversations.

Where cravings whisper.

Where doubt gets loud.

Where grief rearranges the furniture in your chest.

For years, this was my mental battlefield.

When no one was watching, I reached for what numbed instead of what healed.

Bourbon and confession lived here.

Avoidance lived here.

Self-sabotage waited patiently here.

Midnight was where I met the madness that lived in my mind.

The thoughts I had to wrestle.

The urges I had to outthink.

Sometimes the only thing standing between me and self-destruction

was music playing loud enough to keep me here.

Music has been one of my most faithful regulators.

It soothed the chaos.

Cleared the static.

Restored rhythm when my mind lost its beat.

But not every song is safe in every season.

Learning my triggers meant learning that some melodies pull me forward — and others drag me backward.

Midnight taught me discernment.

No one tells you how much insomnia matters.

Bipolar disorder doesn't always show up in fireworks.

Sometimes it walks in dressed as sleeplessness.

At first it's subtle.

A late night here.

A skipped sleep cycle there.

Then your mind starts firing faster than your body can hold.

You feel brilliant. Electric.

Ideas multiply. You clean at 3 a.m.

You reorganize your world.

You call it productivity.

But it's teetering.

Three days without sleep turns clarity into chaos.

There's a fine line between inspiration and instability.

And I've crossed it more than once.

The world romanticizes hustle.

But for someone like me, sleep isn't optional.

It's a life raft.

When sleep forgets you, the body runs on fumes.

The mind becomes a runaway train.

That's where derailment lives.

That's where the fire burns.

So I learned something critical:

Rest is not laziness.

It is recalibration.

Mental endurance costs more than most people understand.

When the mind is depleted, the body always follows.

That's when the warning signs start whispering.

These are the thoughts that surface in the midnight moments:

You replay what you said.

You measure wins and losses.

You question decisions.

You feel pride and disappointment at the same time.

That's not failure.

That's being human.

What matters is this:

There's a difference between listening to your mind

and letting it run you into the ground.

Midnight became my thermostat.

Is my mind overheating — spiraling into regret or panic?

Is it freezing — numb and disconnected?

Is there a storm brewing that needs attention before it becomes destructive?

Your mindset has weather patterns.

Learning to live means learning to read them.

Not to judge them.

But to respond with care.

After the night stops raging, morning still shows up.

And morning requires something different — ritual over ruin.

My rituals are quieter now — small moments of intention and restraint.

Sipping coffee instead of rushing chaos.

Choosing grace before grind.

I've learned that tending to my mind is a holistic act — one that gently stabilizes serotonin instead of demanding productivity before peace.

What once felt like weakness has become wisdom.

In this phase of life, I no longer chase noise or approval. Alignment is my anchor. Peace is my power move.

For a long time, care meant numbing.

Wrong fuel.

And when the wrong fuel meets pain,

you don't get warmth.

You get an explosion.

Alcohol promised relief without requiring presence.

Pills promised silence without healing the noise.

I learned how to function like that.

But coping turned toxic when it became my hiding place.

Stillness without movement isn't peace.

Silence without intention isn't healing.

Sometimes it's avoidance dressed up as strength.

The shift didn't happen in one heroic moment.

It happened quietly.

I had to learn to sit still without anesthetizing myself.

To talk myself down instead of drowning my thoughts.

To ride the wave gently — not become the tidal wave.

Prayer changed too.

Sometimes prayer wasn't asking God to change my life.

It was a whiskey-stained whisper:

God, give me the strength not to destroy my sanity before morning.

And eventually that whisper evolved.

No whiskey.

Just wisdom.

The sounding board that anchors me now is this:

Midnight will always return. Morning isn't the absence of anxiety. It is my answer to it.

Anxiety may knock. It doesn't get to live here.

Triggers change.

Coping evolves.

Strength becomes quieter, not louder.

Empowerment isn't fireworks.

"Still I rise" never meant I felt victorious.

It meant I stayed.

I no longer drown my sorrows in alcohol.

I don't numb the ache to survive the night.

I sit with it.

Aware.

Accountable.

Grounded.

That awareness didn't come overnight.

It came from years of falling apart and rebuilding.

From choosing tools over avoidance.

From letting go of false comforts and earning real peace.

I am scarred gold now.

Not untouched.

Not perfect.

Forged.

Scarred gold doesn't shine because it escaped the fire.

It shines because it survived it.

Midnight draws near.

Not to haunt —

but to close.

Pause.

Before you replay the day.

Before you rewrite the argument.

Before you second-guess the decision.

Take one breath.

You are allowed to end the night

without defending yourself in your own mind.

That's power.

My midnight sessions look different now.

I slow the night down.

I center myself.

I sip serenity instead of chaos.

I release what can be set down before morning.

Music. Breath. Journaling.

Intentional silence.

Sometimes reaching out.

Sometimes simply staying present and letting the moment pass

without destroying myself inside it.

I learned that I don't have to fight my thoughts.

I just have to listen without letting them take over.

As midnight draws near, I return to reflection.

I rest my mind.

I allow stillness to soften what survival hardened.

And when morning comes — clear-headed,

not intoxicated — there is proof.

Proof that restraint is power.

Proof that patience matters.

Proof that healing isn't loud — it's consistent.

As midnight draws near,

I rise —

not as what fear predicted,

not as what addiction tried to claim,

not as what mania once distorted —

but as who I chose to become.

Still here.

Clear-minded.

Grounded.

Scarred gold.

Still rising.

Midnight doesn't make me dramatic anymore.

It makes me deliberate.

There was a time when survival felt like war — loud,
desperate, combustible.

Now it feels different.

Quieter.

Sharper.

Intentional.

This isn't just recovery.

It isn't just reflection.

It's reclamation.

Not a revolution that burns the world down —

but one that rebuilds me from the inside out.

Not chaos.

Not collapse.

Correction.

Because revolution, at its core, isn't noise.

It's decision.

And every night I choose not to self-destruct,

every morning I choose clarity over chaos,

every time I protect my mind instead of punishing it —

that is the fire.

But the discipline?

The pacing?

The restraint?

That's the ice.

And together —

that's how I rise.

I don't run from heat anymore. I choose it.

Growth isn't gentle.

Its scorching ground you cross when something stronger is being forged.

The ground burns when you stop floating.

Clarity has weight.

Forward means friction.

Chapter 23: Crossing the Burning Sands

There comes a point when you stop asking why it happened and start asking how you move forward.

Not loudly.

Not dramatically.

Just with a decision.

I have crossed water.

I have stood in storms.

I have survived tides that tried to claim my name — storms that felt endless.

But sand is different.

Water teaches survival.

Sand demands movement.

But there comes a moment when survival is no longer enough.

There comes a threshold — a burning stretch of ground between who you were and who you are becoming.

That's what this is.

Crossing the burning sands.

Not ceremonial.

Not performative.

Personal.

The sand is hot because growth is uncomfortable.

The ground burns because forward movement requires friction.

Healing is not soft when you are walking barefoot through truth.

Life doesn't move in straight lines.

It moves in tides.

There's glitter and grief in the same breath – one minute you're rising, the next you're swallowing salt.

I stopped trying to outrun the water. I learned to stand in it.

Because the deep end isn't danger.

It's depth.

For a long time, I lived in waves.

Diagnosis.

Shame.

Relapse.

Grief.

Midnight spirals.

Cultural silence.

Every chapter before this one held water.

Unsteady.

Relentless.

Sometimes drowning.

But this part is land.

Solid.

Demanding.

Exposed.

Unforgiving in its clarity.

Because when you step onto sand, you can't blame the current anymore. You have to decide how you will walk.

I learned something after twenty-five years of therapy, soul work, rebuilding, relapsing, returning, relearning:

Momentum over fear.

Not perfection.

Not applause.

Momentum.

Because movement matters more than perfection.

Baby steps are still power.

Tiny shifts are still transformation.

Clarity gets quieter when you stop replaying the past.

Mental backtracking isn't reflection – it's repetition.

It's a loop.

And loops keep you stationary while convincing you you're thinking deeply.

Crossing the burning sands meant refusing to stay stuck in mental quicksand. Life can resemble quicksand. The more you panic, the deeper you sink. The more you thrash, the faster you disappear.

But when you slow down—

when you breathe—

when you shift weight carefully—

you rise.

I have felt lost without my mother.

Felt unanchored.

Unsure of my direction without her mirror holding me steady.

But I am not sinking. I am walking. I have learned which triggers are emergencies. And which are just echoes.

Everything is not a breakdown.

Sometimes it's just life.

Living life on life's terms.

And life does not require dramatics.

It requires discipline.

It requires awareness.

It requires refusing to romanticize chaos.

It requires refusing to self-sabotage at midnight.

For years, I let the diagnosis sit above me like a headline.

But at some point, I stopped accepting it at face value.

I didn't just accept the diagnosis. I interrogated it.

What was chemistry?

What was trauma?

What was inheritance?

And what was simply me?

Education was the key that opened the door for me.

With the right tools, I began to understand what I was actually facing.

Education changed everything.

I started learning about my diagnosis.

I started paying attention to how my mind worked.

I started exploring the tools and paths that could help me live a better life.

The more I learned, the more my perspective shifted.

Knowledge didn't erase the struggle — but it gave me language, clarity, and options.

And that clarity opened the door to freedom.

A lot of people never receive that kind of information.

They don't know what resources exist.

They don't know what questions to ask.

Many people are taught to hide their pain instead of understand it.

One of the most important truths I learned on this journey was simple:

It's okay not to be okay.

And it's okay to seek help.

Some people believe therapy means something is wrong with them.

Others believe medication means weakness.

Some think asking for help means giving up or losing their identity.

None of that is true.

Doing what you need to do to stabilize your life is not weakness.

It is responsibility.

It is survival.

It is strength.

And healing — real healing — is deeply personal.

Healing is your business.

Because the moment you become stagnant—the moment you stop learning, stop moving, stop talking—that's when the real battle is lost. Silence feeds toxicity. Avoidance feeds destruction. When negative thoughts are left unchecked, they take over.

The mind wins that way. Every time.

Movement is resistance. Education is power. Openness is freedom.

Ownership changes everything.

Ownership is friction.

Friction creates heat.

Heat is how you walk the sand without retreating.

Once you question the label, you reclaim the narrative.

And once you reclaim the narrative, movement becomes a choice.

Soul work is showing up for yourself — especially when no one is watching.

Medication can stabilize you.

Therapy can guide you.

Books can inspire you.

But the becoming — the return to yourself — that part belongs to you.

That was the moment my soul opened. Not on a stage. Not in a dramatic breakthrough. But in a quiet realization: no one could do this work for me.

You can receive guidance.

You can hear the language of healing.

But the walk — the real walk — belongs to you.

Soul work begins when excuses end, and responsibility becomes freedom. It requires consistency.

One step at a time.

I am not the woman I was at twenty-two.

I see through a different lens now.

Clearer.

Less frantic.

Less desperate to prove.

More grounded.

More honest.

More responsible for how I speak to myself.

I learned the difference between reflection and rumination.

Between feeling and spiraling.

Between "I'm hurting" and "I am worthless."

It's okay not to be okay.

But it is not okay to punish yourself for being human.

Replacing self-punishment with affirmation changed
everything.

Interrupting the voice that says "I can't"

and answering it with "I'm learning."

That shift is crossing.

That shift is movement.

That shift is sand burning under your feet while you choose
forward anyway.

The greatest comeback isn't to the world.

It's the moment you return to yourself and refuse to retreat.

Crossing the burning sands is not about drama.

It's about direction.

It's about standing firm in your truth.

It's about knowing suicide is never an option—even when the waves feel violent.

It's about choosing to live in the land of the living.

It's about refusing to stay stuck in the middle passage of your own mind.

Water taught me survival. Sand taught me momentum.

And momentum is what carries me forward now.

The sand will always be warm.

Life will always require movement.

But I am no longer afraid of the heat.

Because I know how to walk.

And walking becomes voice.

And voice becomes action.

And action becomes something bigger than survival.

It becomes reclamation.

It belongs to me.

As a Black woman, I learned early how to wear strength before I was ever asked how I felt.

They saw resilience. They didn't see the wounds.

Being labeled bipolar felt like being stamped twice.

Once by society. Once by stigma.

And I refused to let anyone else write my story.

So I dissected it.

What was trauma?

What was legacy?

What was inherited silence?

And what was simply me?

I didn't just accept the diagnosis.

I interrogated it.

Chapter 24: In My Own Name

After they gave me a diagnosis, they gave me definitions before they ever asked who I was.

Bipolar. Addict. Unstable. Too much. Emotional. Difficult.

After more than two decades of carrying what nearly pulled me under, I made a decision.

Not a dramatic declaration. Not a public performance. A private shift.

In my own name.

For years, my name felt attached to explanations.

Some of those words described seasons I survived. None of them defined who I am.

Reclamation is not rebellion.

It is responsibility.

My healing journey did not begin when I was diagnosed. It began when I stopped letting the diagnosis be the loudest voice in the room. I did not just accept it. I interrogated it.

What was chemistry?

What was trauma?

What was grief?

What was inheritance?

What was cultural silence?

What was stigma?

And what was simply me?

The healing journey required education. Not surface-level acceptance. Education.

I learned my triggers. I learned my sleep patterns. I learned how insomnia shifts my mind. I learned what stress does to my emotional framework. I learned that life on life's terms is already hard — and unmanaged mental strain makes it harder.

Therapy helped. Medication helped. Sobriety helped. Journaling helped. Prayer helped. Boundaries helped. Routine helped.

But none of those tools work unless you use them.

That was the turning point.

Healing is not a mood. It is a regimen.

It is tending to your thoughts before they grow wild. It is correcting your internal dialogue. It is saying, "This spiral stops here." It is recognizing when your mind is overheating. It is knowing when to rest. It is knowing when to ask for help. It is knowing when silence is strength — and when silence is avoidance.

For a long time, I thought strength meant endurance — how much I could absorb without breaking, how much I could hide without being questioned.

But containment is not healing.

Staying functional is not the same thing as being well.

My healing journey required structure.

Governance entered when I realized something simple:

If I don't govern my mind, it will govern me.

Governance is not control born of fear. It is stewardship born of awareness.

It meant no longer romanticizing chaos. No longer glorifying emotional intensity. No longer mistaking instability for depth.

It meant seeing myself clearly.

It meant understanding that I am not my diagnosis. I am not a prisoner of my mind. I am not obligated to live inside stigma. I am not required to wear labels like permanent identity.

Therapy gave me language. Medication gave me stability. Sobriety gave me clarity. Soul work gave me reflection.

But responsibility gave me authority.

This is what people don't talk about enough:

You can have all the tools in the world, and still stay stagnant if you refuse to move.

Mental paralysis doesn't always look dramatic. Sometimes it looks like overthinking. Replaying. Reliving. Rehashing. Convincing yourself you're processing when you're actually looping.

Healing interrupts that.

Healing asks: Are you moving forward? Or are you circling the same wound with new vocabulary?

Life on life's terms is hard. Grief is hard. Sobriety is hard. Managing mood is hard. Living as a Black woman under both expectation and stereotype is hard.

But stagnation is harder.

Because stagnation turns the mind into quicksand. And the more you thrash inside your thoughts, the deeper you sink.

The healing journey required daily decision. Not once. Daily.

Not perfection. Consistency.

Not applause. Discipline.

Not performance. Ownership.

Ownership of how I speak to myself. Ownership of what I feed my mind. Ownership of what I call truth. Ownership of what I refuse to accept about myself anymore.

Containment is not the same thing as healing.

Reclaiming my name did not end the struggle.

It redirected it.

It shifted me from reaction to responsibility.

It shifted me from coping to stewardship.

And that shift gave language to what I once called revolution.

Healing Is My Revolution

My healing didn't come wrapped in pretty packages or softly lit therapy rooms.

It didn't come with a manual either.

It came with shame.

Side-eyes.

Labels whispered like verdicts.

Fear that sat in my chest longer than hope.

It came in midnight sobs.

In overdoses I wasn't supposed to survive.

In hospital rooms where hope was flat lining — where machines measured what I could not control, where the air smelled sterile and prayer wasn't poetic, it was desperate.

It came in prayers I didn't think were heard.

In days I didn't think I'd see the sunrise again.

But I'm still here.

I'm here because I got tired of suffering in silence.

Tired of being the strong one in public and falling apart behind closed doors.

Tired of building walls instead of building bridges — to myself, to my son, to a future I could actually see — and want to live in.

Healing is not cute.

It is not trendy.

It is not for show.

It is gritty.

It is raw.

It is the quiet war between the version trauma shaped in darkness and the version of me that refused to disappear.

Knowledge became my power. Education became my strategy. Therapy became reinforcement. Sobriety became clarity.

Soul work became reconstruction — the steady rebuilding of a mind I once let unravel.

I learned the tactics of isolation — the whisper that says withdraw, the lie that says disappear, the suggestion that silence is safer.

Silence almost kept me.

That is why healing became my revolution. Not because it was loud. But because it interrupted what was quietly destroying me. Revolution, for me, was interruption.

Interrupting the spiral before it hardened into identity.

Interrupting inherited silence before it defined my future.

Interrupting the narrative that predicted my collapse.

Eventually healing stopped looking like survival

and started looking like discipline.

It looked like keeping appointments when shame wanted me home.

Choosing sobriety when numbness felt easier.

Tracking triggers instead of ignoring them.

Resting before collapse instead of after.

Healing was not aesthetic. It was maintenance.

Small corrections.

Repeated alignment.

Steady structure.

Not destruction.

Reconstruction.

That is where sovereignty became real.

Not in the shouting.

In the showing up.

In my own name, I refused to be governed by stigma.

In my own name, I refused paralysis.

In my own name, I chose structure over chaos and claimed authority over how I respond to what I feel.

My revolution was not about burning anything down.

It was about rebuilding — deliberately. And rebuilding takes tools.

Responsibility replaced rebellion.

Structure replaced survival.

Stewardship replaced chaos.

And stewardship is power.

Healing did not make me flawless. It made me accountable.

Accountable for my triggers.

Accountable for my boundaries.

Accountable for my discipline.

Accountable for my peace.

Reclaiming my name did not finish my journey.

It clarified it.

In my own name, I stopped fighting for survival and started building for stability.

And real building takes time.

Structure. Patience. Revision.

Not perfection — intention.

Not polish — persistence.

Not completion — commitment.

Deliberate work, sustained over time, becomes art.

This is how I understand myself now.

Not as broken. Not diminished.

Becoming.

A masterpiece in progress.

Mental health is not entertainment. It is lived experience.

"Normal" and "crazy" are stories we inherit, not truths we choose.

Therapy helped me understand.

Recovery helped me stabilize.

But soul work helped me remember who I was when language ran out.

What survived the fire did not disappear.

It became scarred gold.

Chapter 25: Masterpiece in Progress

There were years that tried to define me in permanent ink.

Diagnosis. Detour. Collapse. Recovery.

But none of those words finished the sentence.

I am not the sharpest moment of my unraveling.

I am not the cleanest chapter of my rebuilding.

I am the woman who kept becoming.

That is the difference.

You can only be reduced so many times before you decide to define

yourself.

That was the turning point.

Not the diagnosis. Not the relapse. Not the setbacks.

The decision to stand in my own name.

Everything before this shaped me—

but it does not contain me.

I am no longer negotiating my existence.

I am no longer adjusting my presence to make it easier to swallow.

I do not end where I began.

That matters.

Some lives are measured in milestones.

Mine was measured in return.

Return to myself.

Return to discipline.

Return after regret.

Return after damage.

Again. And again.

That repetition did not weaken me. It trained me.

There is nothing fragile about evolution.

It is relentless.

It strips illusion.

It burns pride.

It exposes truth.

And then it asks—will you stay?

I did.

I have lived through volatility.

Through silence.

Through collapse and return.

What remained is not fragile.

It is focused.

There is depth in me that did not exist before.

Not dramatic depth. Not chaos.

Measured.

I understand the architecture of my own mind now.

My thresholds. My patterns. My power.

That awareness is not heavy anymore.

It is leverage.

I am not rushing to escape my history.

I am standing firmly inside it.

I do not romanticize what hurt me.

But I do not shrink from what it built in me either.

This life has required endurance.

It has required discipline.

It has required more from me than I thought I had.

But here I am.

Not polished into perfection.

Not healed into silence.

Integrated.

Layered.

Present.

I am not defined by collapse.

I am defined by continuity.

By staying.

By returning.

By choosing again when it would have been easier not to.

I am not racing toward completion.

Completion is a myth.

Growth is structure under pressure.

And I am structured now.

Not rigid.

Composed.

There are layers in me now that did not exist at twenty-two:

Restraint.

Patience.

Discernment.

Authority.

I did not become smaller.

I became precise.

If this book proves anything, it proves this:

You can fracture.

You can fall.

You can miscalculate.

You can lose.

You can grieve.

And still refuse to disappear.

The masterpiece is not perfection.

It is persistence with awareness.

My story is not finished. It isn't supposed to be.

I am not a cautionary tale.

I am not a polished redemption arc.

I am living proof of endurance.

This is not the end of my becoming—

but it is the end of my doubt about who I am.

I am steady enough to grow.

Strong enough to revise.

Clear enough to move forward without apology.

And there is something quieter than confidence that lives here now.

It is presence.

I do not enter spaces asking to be understood.

I enter as someone who understands herself.

I no longer measure my value against reaction.

I measure it against alignment.

There is no urgency in me to convince.

No pressure to perform recovery.

No need to dramatize progress.

The proof is in the posture.

In the way I carry calm without tension.

In the way I speak without bracing.

In the way I allow silence to sit without scrambling to fill it.

This is not spectacle.

It is integration.

And integration has weight.

What stands here now is not fragile.

Not frantic. Not performing.

But fire —

tempered by heat,

shaped by pressure,

and still burning on purpose.

CODA: Scarred Gold

From the Author's Desk

What you are about to read is not a conclusion.

It is a continuation.

Scarred Gold was born in fire — not metaphorical fire, but lived heat.

Pressure.

Time.

Damage that did not destroy — only refine.

I didn't survive in spite of the fire.

I survived because of it.

Pressure shaped me.

Heat refined me.

I emerged — scarred gold.

This is not the end of *Whiskey Prayers and Midnight Moments*.

It is the beginning of what comes next.

The continuation is coming.

Scarred Gold

The trifecta of healing: raw reflection, inner truth, and self-discovery.

This is a spoken truth forged in lived experience.

Bipolar disorder.

PTSD.

Trauma.

Alcoholism.

Alcohol was my fiercest beast.

For twenty-five years, I lived in survival mode — inside diagnosis,

stigma, and a nervous system wired for chaos. I wear my scars like

earned currency.

Not shame.

Not weakness.

Proof.

Proof I lived.

Proof I endured.

Proof what tried to destroy me did not win.

Suicidal ideation.

Attempts.

An emptiness so deep that existing felt unbearable.

The heat was real.

The damage was real.

But so was the forging.

Where the world saw ruin, a different process was unfolding. Under

pressure, metal strengthens. Under fire, ore separates from impurity.

What appears to be destruction is often refinement in motion.

This is metallurgy of the soul.

Gold does not become gold without flame.

Neither did I.

Alcohol promised relief and delivered wreckage. It stripped me to the

bone, exposed fracture, forced truth into the open. But what survived

the furnace did not dissolve — it condensed.

Structure formed in the cracks.

Density replaced collapse.

Weak metal burns off. What remains holds.

This is not glamorized suffering.

This is transformation under heat.

Healing is not pretty. It's precise.

Repetitive.

Earned.

It asks you to stay long after the spectacle fades

—

after chaos quiets —

after the noise stops entertaining you.

That is the sweet spot.

Not just survival

Stability.

When pain loosens its grip.

When memory stops bleeding.

When the nervous system exhales without bracing for impact.

People see the shine.

They do not see the furnace.

They do not see the slow refinement.

The discipline required to remain whole.

Whiskey Prayers and Midnight Moments was forged there —

in wreckage, in heat, in refusal.

Not polished perfection. Tempered truth.

I did not survive in spite of the fire.

I survived because of it.

Pressure shaped me.

Heat clarified me.

I emerged—

Scarred Gold.

Epilogue

Let's not romanticize this.

I did not survive because I was strong. I survived because I refused to vanish.

There were years my own mind tried to outvote me. Years when the diagnosis tried to become identity. Years I could have let the label write the ending.

It didn't.

Not because I was graceful.

Because I was unwilling.

I have worn scarlet letters. I have swallowed stigma. I have stood in rooms shrinking myself so other people could stay comfortable.

I don't do that anymore.

Healing did not make me softer.

It made me sharper.

It made me selective.

It made me disciplined.

It made me intolerant of anything that destabilizes what I fought to rebuild.

I don't overexplain. I don't beg to be understood. I don't grant access to what agitates my nervous system.

Not because I'm fragile.

Because I remember the collapse.

I remember the cost.

You think survival is enduring everything.

It's not.

Survival, when it grows up, becomes refusal.

Refusal to self-abandon. Refusal to return to chaos. Refusal to let instability become personality.

I built this mind back brick by brick.

I fought for regulation when unraveling would have been easier. I chose participation when disappearing felt seductive. I chose boundaries when tolerance would have looked nicer.

I did not walk away from this story polished.

I walked away precise.

Steady. Watchful. Deliberate.

The victory is not applause.

It's waking up in a body that doesn't feel at war.

It's peace you defend. Structure you maintain. Fire you control.

I am not what almost ended me.

I am what survived it — and what burned the weak parts off.

Not surviving chaos.

Rising through it.

Support and Recovery Resources

These tools are not just ideas — they are weapons, lifelines, anchors. They are proof that healing is possible. That mental health management is not just possible — it's powerful.

These tools saved me. And now they live here, in these pages, to help someone else survive too.

Mental health toolbox:

1. SAMHSA Helpline —

1-800-662-HELP (4357)

Free, 24/7 Support for mental health and substance use challenges.

1. NAMI (National Alliance on Mental Illness) – nami.org

Education, support groups, and resources for individuals and families.

1. PsychologyToday.com

Search and connect with local licensed therapists in your area.

1. PHP/IOP Programs

Partial hospitalization and intensive outpatient programs critical for support without full hospitalization.

1. Crisis Text Line- Text 741741

Free, confidential help

1. Suicide and Crisis Lifeline- call or text 988

24/7, Nationwide support for those in crisis.

Everyone with bipolar experiences it differently. No two lives are the same. So, I had to figure out how it affects me. That's how I learned how to prepare, adjust, and respond. It's not perfect. But it's power.

Acknowledgements

This season of my life is quiet and intentional. I am more private now. More protective. More grounded.

Still, growth is never as solitary as it feels.

To the loved ones who stood with me — sometimes close, sometimes at a distance — thank you. Your presence mattered more than you know.

To the professionals who offered language, structure, and truth when everything felt unstable — thank you. Guidance and accountability helped shape this path.

To the spiritual voices who reminded me that faith and psychology do not compete — thank you. Recovery did not shrink my life. It strengthened it.

The healing work itself was personal.

Soul work is daily — tending the mind, guarding peace, choosing growth.

To those who walked even part of this road beside me — thank you for witnessing the becoming.

— JAI Lewis

Meet the Author

JAI Lewis

About the Author

JAI Lewis is a memoirist whose work explores the intersection of mental health, addiction recovery, faith, and identity. Her work is grounded in decades of navigating bipolar disorder, cultural silence, self-advocacy, and the daily discipline of stability.

Raised in an educated family unprepared for the complexities of a psychiatric diagnosis, she learned in real time what recovery requires — not just understanding, but participation. Over the years, through therapy, treatment, and what she calls "soul work," she rebuilt her relationship with her mind, her body, and her life.

Whiskey Prayers and Midnight Moments is her debut memoir. She is currently working on her next book, Scarred Gold.

Live. Strive. Thrive

-JAI Lewis

Book Club Invitation

Thank you for reading *Whiskey Prayers and Midnight Moments*.

If your book club selects this memoir, I would love to hear about your conversation and reflections. This story was written not just to be read, but to spark honest dialogue about healing, mental health, resilience, and the power of rebuilding a life.

Readers and book clubs are welcome to share their discussions and thoughts online using the hashtag #WhiskeyPrayers.

Your voices, stories, and perspectives help keep the conversation going.